Walking in the Word

Fifty Daily Devotions to Deepen Your Relationship with God

Leon R. Gooden, Jr.

sermontobook.com

Sermon To Book
www.sermontobook.com

Walking in the Word / Leon R. Gooden, Jr.
ISBN-13: 978-1-945793-09-7
ISBN-10: 1-945793-09-0

First, I would like to give God all the glory for giving me the understanding of His Word to be able to complete this project.

Second, I would like to thank my lovely wife and co-laborer in the Lord's church, Pastor Jennifer D. Gooden for her support and prayers for this project—as well my three children, Damien, Leon III, and India.

Third, I would like to thank the entire Kingdom Builders Christian Ministries, International, for allowing for me to be your Senior Pastor for the past six years.

And last but not least, I would like to thank Chief Apostle Alvin and Pastor Jacque McCullough from Manna From Heaven Ministries, International, for their spiritual covering and love.

I pray all who would read this book be richly blessed.

To God be the Glory!

CONTENTS

INTRODUCTION

Welcome to *Walking in the Word*

In this day and age, truth appears to be opinion. What is right for one person is wrong for another. Black is white, right is wrong, left is right! Even Christians seem to struggle with finding a measuring stick for truth. Paul spoke about what people would be like in this day in 2 Timothy 3:7, saying they would be "always learning and never able to arrive at a knowledge of the truth" (ESV). The Bible says in the last days before Christ's return false prophets will come to tickle people's ears, telling them what they want to hear (2 Timothy 4:3) but mixing truth with lies. Sounds like this generation, doesn't it?

It is critical that believers cling to God's Word as their only source of truth because the enemy is subtle and deceiving. He wants to confuse, tear down and immobilize God's people, convincing them truth is relative and God is absent. However, God is not a God of disorder, but of peace (1 Corinthians 14:33). He is very present, never leaving those He loves. He promises to reveal "deep and hidden things" for those who seek Him (Daniel 2:22). In fact, Paul encouraged first-century believers, and thus believers today, to "Think over what I say, for the Lord will give you understanding in everything" (2 Timothy 2:7).

I wrote *Walking in the Word* to encourage and challenge those who are growing weary in this hour, who are diligently fighting their battles each day but need a dose of truth to fill them up before they step back out into the war.

Each chapter is a Scripture-based mini-lesson that is a cross between a devotional and a Bible study. Many chapters include a look into the Greek or Hebrew meaning of words to help shed light on God's intended meaning of certain passages. You will be encouraged with such topics as being called by God, standing firm in the battle against enemies, choosing to be part of God's plan, and being empowered to be a witness to Christ. Each one- to three-page chapter is short enough to be read when you don't have much time but still deeply challenging and convicting. My hope is readers will find truth "nuggets" in each chapter that will remain with them throughout their day and week, and even their life.

Leon R. Gooden, Jr., 2016

CHAPTER ONE

In God's Economy, Age Doesn't Matter

A child would *never* be elected president, right? But in 641 BC in ancient Israel, a young boy was given the highest position of authority over the people—Josiah, the son of King Amon and Jedidah, was crowned king at just eight years old!

God calls every person who puts their faith in Jesus to become actively involved in His purposes and plans for the world. Often, however, people are hesitant to begin serving God and others because they think they are not "mature" enough—either because they are young in age, or young in understanding of God's Word.

But to God, age and spiritual maturity are not deterrents! The Lord can use anyone—whether they accepted Jesus five minutes ago or fifty years ago.

Consider what God said of Josiah's ability to be a king:

Josiah was eight years old when he became king, and he reigned in Jerusalem thirty-one years. He did what was right in the eyes of the Lord and followed the ways of his father David, not turning aside to the right or to the left.

> *In the eighth year of his reign, while he was still young, he began to seek the God of his father David. In his twelfth year he began to purge Judah and Jerusalem of high places, Asherah poles and idols. —* ***2 Chronicles 34:3 (NIV)***

Josiah may have been a child, but that didn't deter God from using Him. Notice what the writer of 2 Chronicles said about Josiah: "He did what was right in the eyes of the LORD and followed the ways of his father David, not turning aside to the right or the left" (2 Chronicles 34:2 NIV). When did He start following the Lord? The answer comes in the next verse: "In the eighth year of his reign…" (2 Chronicles 34:3 NIV).

Eight years after becoming King—when he was only sixteen years old—Josiah began following the Lord. The kingdom he inherited was crumbling. On top of that, both his father and grandfather were two of the most wicked kings in Judah's history. In spite of this, this teenager purged Judah of idol worship, and followed God.

There is a wonderful lesson in this story of Josiah. Serving is not only for adults, and it's not only for those who have been following Jesus for many years. It's not reserved for those who come from perfect spiritual families, or for those who have a staff position at a church. Josiah didn't fit any of those molds, and God chose him to lead His most treasured possession—Israel!

The prophet Micah reveals what God asks of those who follow Him: "And what does the LORD require of you? To act justly and to love mercy and to *walk humbly with your God*" (Micah 6:8 NIV, emphasis added).

God doesn't necessitate a resume laden with years of experience leading large ministries in an established, well-known church to serve Him. He requires humble faith, and the commitment to follow Jesus wherever He leads. The moment you put your faith in Christ, you are given everything you need for spiritual maturity—whether you are a brand new believer, or you have been following Jesus for forty years.

CHAPTER TWO

A Place for Trembling

Therefore, my dear friends, as you have always obeyed—not only in my presence, but now much more in my absence—continue to work out your salvation with fear and trembling. ***— Philippians 2:12 (NIV)***

Why is it so easy for people to focus on the "softer" side of God? Perhaps it feels safe to concentrate on some of God's more appealing characteristics—His love, mercy and grace, for example—and avoid God's righteous indignation, holiness, justice, and punishment for sin. The wrathful, powerful and just side of God is cast aside for what is comfortable. People pick and choose what parts of God they want.

The concept of coming before God with fear and trembling is certainly not popular. However, in Philippians 2:2, Paul said this is exactly how we should approach God—and it is actually a beautiful thing!

The word 'fear' in Philippians 2 is the word *phobos*, and it is described as "reverence" and "a sense of awe."[1] How do reverence and awe connect with 'trembling'? Those words almost seem to contradict. 'Trembling' is the Greek word *tromos*, meaning "quaking with fear" or "the anxiety of one who distrusts his ability completely to meet all requirements, but religiously does his utmost to fulfil his duty."[2]

In the Old Testament, Psalm 33:8–9 says, "Let all the earth fear the LORD; Let all the inhabitants of the world stand in awe of Him. For He spoke, and it was done; He commanded, and it stood fast" (NASB). Here the word 'fear' is the Hebrew word *yirah,* and though this word can mean "fear" or "terror," it also means respect, "reverence" or "piety."[3]

Fearing God does not mean being scared of God. God by His very nature is love, peace, joy, and kindness. Exodus 34:6-7 says, "The LORD, the LORD God, merciful and gracious, longsuffering, and abounding in goodness and truth…" (NKJV). However, these verses also say He will punish the wicked; God's goodness will manifest itself in wrathful justice against those who are against God and choose evil. Knowing this, there is a proper posture the believer must have standing before this holy, sovereign, perfect God.

An appropriate fear of the Lord, then, would include reverence and awe—not wanting to offend God in any way. It is the knowledge of who God is, and deciding that He is the most important thing in all of life. It is "quaking with awe and reverence" When this knowledge is embraced, it results in many positive things in the believer's life! Scripture says, "The fear of the LORD is the beginning of knowledge…" (Proverbs 1:7 NKJV); it is the key to wisdom. When a person's posture before God is one of awe and reverence, they naturally hate evil (Proverbs 8:13) and are filled with a supernatural, strong confidence that is Christ—the fountain of life (Proverbs 14:26–27). As Proverbs 22:4 tells us, "the fear of the LORD are riches and honor and life" (NKJV).

There is a place for trembling before God, and it is a good and safe place. Only the person who humbly stands before the Lord awe and reverence has God's promise to receive His everlasting tender love:

> *But the lovingkindness of the LORD is from everlasting to everlasting on those who fear Him...* — ***Psalm 103:17 (NASB)***

CHAPTER THREE

The Spoken Word—God's "Hammer"

So shall My word be that goes forth from My mouth; it shall not return to Me void, but it shall accomplish what I please, and it shall prosper in the thing for which I sent it.
— Isaiah 55:11 (NKJV)

Theologian A.W. Tozer writes:

> The Bible is the written word of God, and because it is written it is confined and limited by the necessities of ink and paper and leather. The Voice of God, however, is alive and free as the sovereign God is free. … The life is in the speaking words. God's word in the Bible can have power only because it corresponds to God's word in the universe. It is the present Voice which makes the written Word all-powerful. Otherwise it would lie locked in slumber within the covers of a book.[4]

But in Isaiah 55:1, the prophet said God's Word had to be released for it to have power. Once released, it accomplished God's intended purpose for it. It created the universe, the heavens, the seas, people, and animals. God's spoken word is so powerful it creates life! There is irresistible supernatural power in God's Word; it will not return to Him empty. It will get the job done!

In the same way, the believer's spoken word has power when it is God's Word spoken in faith through their lips.

The prophet Jeremiah said:

> *The prophet who has a dream, let him tell a dream; and he who has My word, let him speak My word faithfully. What is the chaff to the wheat?" says the LORD. "Is not My word like a fire?" says the LORD, "And like a hammer that breaks the rock in pieces?"* — ***Jeremiah 23:28 (NKJV)***

When the believer speaks God's Word faithfully, the Bible says it is like a hammer that can break rocks. The apostle Paul encourages believers, "The word is near you, in your mouth and in your heart (that is, the word of faith which we preach)..." (Romans 10:8 NKJV). It is not something we have to go and find; it is with us all the time. And the writer of Hebrews said, "The word of God is living and powerful, and sharper than any two-edged sword, piercing even to the division of soul and spirit, and of joints and marrow, and is a discerner of the thoughts and intents of the heart" (Hebrews 4:12 NKJV).

God's Word is so powerful and so intensely sharp it can set people free from addictive behaviors, from temptation, and from sin. It can heal illnesses and realign finances. It can make a person holy, sanctified. It can raise the dead to life! Jesus said, "The words that I speak to you are spirit, and they are life" (John 6:63 NKJV). Therefore, if we have hidden God's Word in our hearts (Psalm 119:11), we too can speak those same words and bring life from the dead—eternal life in Jesus Christ.

The all-powerful Word of God, "the word of faith," is in your heart and mouth to be spoken. This "hammer" can move obstacles, overcome negatives, and pull down strongholds. Speak it! It will never return void!

Sanctify them by Your truth. Your word is truth. — ***John 17:17 (NKJV)***

CHAPTER FOUR

Don't Turn Back

For we will destroy this place, because the outcry against them has grown great before the face of the LORD, and the Lord has sent us to destroy it." So Lot went out and spoke to his sons-in-law, who had married his daughters, and said, "Get up, get out of this place; for the LORD will destroy this city!" But to his sons-in-law he seemed to be joking. When the morning dawned, the angels urged Lot to hurry, saying, "Arise, take your wife and your two daughters who are here, lest you be consumed in the punishment of the city." And while he lingered, the men took hold of his hand, his wife's hand, and the hands of his two daughters, the LORD being merciful to him, and they brought him out and set him outside the city. So it came to pass, when they had brought them outside, that he said, "Escape for your life! Do not look behind you nor stay anywhere in the plain. Escape to the mountains, lest you be destroyed." ***— Genesis 19:13–17 (NKJV)***

The sun had risen upon the earth when Lot entered Zoar. Then the LORD rained brimstone and fire on Sodom and Gomorrah, from the LORD out of the heavens. So He overthrew those cities, all the plain, all the inhabitants of the cities, and what grew on the ground. But his wife looked back behind him, and she became a pillar of salt.

— Genesis 19:23–26 (NKJV)

In Genesis 19, God sent two angels to Lot to tell him to get out of Sodom and Gomorrah because He was going to demolish the city. So Lot told his wife, his daughters, and their husbands—all of whom thought it was a joke—they needed to flee. When morning came they set out, but Lot's wife looked back—and was transformed into a pillar of salt!

Sodom and Gomorrah had become so corrupt that its people had lost any sense of conviction for sexual and moral sin, and ultimately the city was destroyed because of it. God was calling Lot and his family out of Sodom and Gomorrah; He was calling them to change. Lot's wife left with the family and was told not to even look back at Sodom and Gomorrah. Unfortunately, she chose to look back, and it destroyed her.

Shifting and changing are two different things!

Lot's wife "shifted," but she didn't change, and it cost her life. She shifted locations but didn't change her mindset. The Bible says believers are changed into a "new creation" (2 Corinthians 5:17 NKJV) when they believe in Jesus: "Therefore, if anyone is in Christ, he is a new creation; old things have passed away; behold, all things have become new" (2 Corinthians 5:17 NKJV).

Shifting and changing, though two different things, go hand in hand. To "shift" is to cause something or someone to move. To "change" is to cause someone or something to be different. A person can shift (move) but not change. But the apostolic call on the believer's life require both a shift *and* a change—He calls His people to turn from sin (shift) and to repent (change).

Satan will be close behind, speaking untruth into the ears of the believer. God may tell you to move somewhere, to speak to someone, to make a lifestyle change or to flat out turn from sin. But Satan may be whispering, "God didn't really mean what He said," or "God wouldn't really want you to change that." John 10:10a says, "The thief does not come except to steal, and to kill, and to destroy" (NKJV). Jesus, however, said that He has "come that they may have life, and that they may have it more abundantly" (John 10:10b NKJV).

Stay focused! Be direct and of good courage. God is inviting His people to move with Him. When He does, don't turn back. Press on toward the restoration God has waiting for those He loves.

> *I press on toward the goal to win the prize for which God has called me heavenward in Christ Jesus.* — ***Philippians 3:14 (NIV)***

CHAPTER FIVE

You Are a Child of God

There is therefore now no condemnation to those who are in Christ Jesus, who do not walk according to the flesh, but according to the Spirit. — ***Romans 8:1 (NKJV)***

Did you know there is a distinction between sin and guilt? Sin is objective—it is not dependent on a person's mind. But guilt is *subjective*—it is reliant on the mind. Guilt is what a person feels inside because of sin.

One of Satan's main tactics is playing on the mind, and making people feel guilty or ashamed. According to the Bible, Satan is the accuser of God's people, "who accused them before our God day and night…" (Revelation 12:10 NKJV).

However, those who have received Jesus as Lord and Savior do not stand accused, "by the blood of the Lamb and by the word of their testimony" (Revelation 12:11 NKJV). Knowing this, it is paramount that believers stand on the Word of God and what it says about the power in Christ's death and resurrection.

Jesus' death redeems believers from slavery: "In Him we have redemption through His blood, the forgiveness of sins, according to the riches of His grace" (Ephesians 1:7 NKJV). As we walk in the light and have fellowship with one another, His blood continually cleanses us from sin: "But if we walk in the light, as He is in the light, we have fellowship with one another, and the blood of Jesus Christ His Son cleanses us from all sin" (1 John 1:7 NKJV)

Guilt is what a person feels inside because of sin. It could be a past failure, a religious background that emphasized converting from sin rather than conversion to Christ, or people who were critical and condemnatory. However, the moment a person believes on Jesus, Romans 5:9 says, "Much more then, having now been justified by His blood, we shall be saved from wrath through Him" (NKJV). In a legal sense, they were acquitted of the crime of sinning against God! Hebrews 13:12 says Jesus sanctified the people "with His own blood" (NKJV)—that is, He made them holy—and brought them near to God once again so that they might boldly enter His presence (Hebrews 10:19–22).

"Therefore there is now no condemnation for those who are in Christ Jesus." (Romans 8:1 NASB). In fact, Scripture says that instead of shame and condemnation, the believer has received "double honor":

> *Instead of your shame you shall have double honor, and instead of confusion they shall rejoice in their portion. Therefore in their land they shall possess double; everlasting joy shall be theirs.* ***—Isaiah 61:7 (NKJV)***

Dr. Les Parrot writes, "Shame is a spin-off from guilt. We may feel guilty for what we did, but we feel ashamed of who we are."[5] If you struggle with shame and guilt, meditate on verses that remind you of what (and whose) you *really* are: God's child, accepted and highly favored, and made holy and righteous by the blood of Jesus! You no longer are in a place of sin and shame, but stand in the light, forgiven and pure in God's eyes.

> *For He made Him who knew no sin to be sin for us, that we might become the righteousness of God in Him.* ***—2 Corinthians 5:21 (NKJV)***

CHAPTER SIX

Run with the Vision

Then I said to them, "You see the distress that we are in, how Jerusalem lies waste, and its gates are burned with fire. Come and let us build the wall of Jerusalem, that we may no longer be a reproach." — ***Nehemiah 2:17 (NKJV)***

Nehemiah was a prophet who was instrumental in rebuilding and reestablishing Jerusalem after the Babylonian exile in the fifth century BC. The Israelites had been given the freedom to leave Babylon and return to Jerusalem, but the city was in shambles. Picture Nehemiah walking around the ruins, looking at his beloved city—its gates charred and stones toppled one on top of another on the ground—and crying out to God in his heart: *What should I do?*

Notice in Nehemiah 2:17, Scripture says Nehemiah responded to what he saw by saying to the officials and Jews, "Come and let us build the wall of Jerusalem..." (Nehemiah 2:17 NKJV). What he saw deeply affected him, but he didn't turn a blind eye. Rather, he perceived there was work to be done. There was rebuilding to do—and he leaned into that vision.

Merriam-Webster's Learner's Dictionary defines vision as (1) "the ability to see: sight or eyesight"; (2) "something you imagine: a picture you see in your mind"; or (3) "something you see or dream especially as part of a religious or supernatural experience."[6]

Nehemiah remembered what Jerusalem used to be, was broken and humbled by what it now was, and was moved to restore the city and bring hope to a hopeless people.

God allows us to "see" things and moves our hearts to align with His—but the key element is response. We must take a step out and trust God for the vision He has put in our heart. Indeed, the book of Proverbs teaches us, "Where there is no vision, the people perish: but he that keepeth the law, happy is he" (Proverbs 29:18 KJV).

Nehemiah 1:4 says that when Nehemiah realized the condition of Jerusalem, he "sat down and wept, and mourned for many days; I was fasting and praying before the God of heaven" (NKJV). When God allows you to "see" something with pure eyes, a vision of what He wants done, and if it breaks your heart to where you know you can't sit back and do nothing, don't be afraid to come alongside what He is already doing and take part in something beyond yourself.

And know with confidence that as insurmountable as the vision may seem, Jesus promises that He will never leave or forsake you. In Christ, you can move even the biggest mountain!

For assuredly, I say to you, whoever says to this mountain, 'Be removed and be cast into the sea,' and does not doubt in his heart, but believes that those things he says will be done, he will have whatever he says. Therefore I say to you, whatever things you ask when you pray, believe that you receive them, and you will have them. — ***Mark 11:23–24 (NKJV)***

CHAPTER SEVEN

Pursue Your Miracle

Now it happened, on a certain day, that He got into a boat with His disciples. And He said to them, "Let us cross over to the other side of the lake." And they launched out. But as they sailed He fell asleep. And a windstorm came down on the lake, and they were filling with water, and were in jeopardy. And they came to Him and awoke Him, saying, "Master, Master, we are perishing!" Then He arose and rebuked the wind and the raging of the water. And they ceased, and there was a calm. But He said to them, "Where is your faith?" And they were afraid, and marveled, saying to one another, "Who can this be? For He commands even the winds and water, and they obey Him!" ***—Luke 8:22–25 (NKJV)***

More often than not, when a believer is called to "go" there is almost surely a storm ahead of any miracle. Often, it is to test or strengthen one's faith. When the believer is given a word from the Lord, the enemy likes nothing more than to twist the instruction God has given to cause doubt or even fear. Step out courageously, knowing God will never leave or forsake those He calls!

Consider Joshua. God called this young man to lead an entire nation into the Promised Land. Joshua was Moses' second in command. Though he was considered one of the greatest military leaders in human history, his military genius was not his own! Exodus 17:3 reveals the only reason Joshua squashed the Amalekites in battle was because "Moses held up his hand" (Exodus 17:11 NKJV).

> *...Israel prevailed; and when he let down his hand, Amalek prevailed.* ***— Exodus 17:11 (NKJV)***

God—the true Commander in Chief—was responsible for Joshua's victory on the battlefield. Years later, after Moses died and Joshua was installed as leader, God commanded Joshua to lead Israel across the Jordan River and the land promised to Israel. God exhorted Joshua, saying, "Have I not commanded you? Be strong and of good courage; do not be afraid, nor be dismayed, for the LORD your God is with you wherever you go" (NKJV).

Joshua obeyed, but he faced not just one but many storms before God's promise was fulfilled—He fought for seven years before conquering the land! However, the miracle promised did indeed come to pass. The victory was won before Joshua even put one toe in the waters of the Jordan River. God only required Joshua step out in faith and face the storms. God would fight the battle.

Miracles in Scripture didn't come to people standing still, doing nothing, and sitting on their gift; they happened through people who stepped out in faith—even if it was blind faith! In the same way, miracles don't happen today through individuals who are comfortable, complacent, satisfied with where they are or are expecting/wanting nothing. Success comes for the child of God who believes God at His Word and responds.

In Luke 8:22–25, Jesus commanded His disciples to "cross over to the other side of the lake…" (Luke 8:22 NKJV) knowing there was a storm ahead. When waves and wind raged, and the disciples panicked, Jesus reprimanded them, saying, "Where is your faith?" (Luke 8:25 NKJV)

Don't sit back and wait. Trust God, face potential storms, and get up and go! Your miracle is waiting on you!

You are the God who performs miracles; you display your power among the peoples. — ***Psalm 77:14 (NIV)***

CHAPTER EIGHT

See and Be Filled Again

And Ananias went his way and entered the house; and laying his hands on him he said, "Brother Saul, the Lord Jesus, who appeared to you on the road as you came, has sent me that you may receive your sight and be filled with the Holy Spirit." Immediately there fell from his eyes something like scales, and he received his sight at once; and he arose and was baptized. So when he had received food, he was strengthened. Then Saul spent some days with the disciples at Damascus. Immediately he preached the Christ in the synagogues, that He is the Son of God. Then all who heard were amazed, and said, "Is this not he who destroyed those who called on this name in Jerusalem, and has come here for that purpose, so that he might bring them bound to the chief priests?" But Saul increased all the more in strength, and confounded the Jews who dwelt in Damascus, proving that this Jesus is the Christ. — ***Acts 9:17–22 (NKJV)***

Acts 9 speaks of two New Testament characters, Ananias and Saul. Saul, notorious for persecuting Christians, had departed Jerusalem after obtaining a letter granting him authority to arrest any Christians he could find in Damascus. He was to bring those believers to Jerusalem for trial before the puppet court of the Sanhedrin. But lo and behold, while on the road to Damascus, he had a dramatic, life-changing conversion experience. Out of a shining light Jesus called to him and said "Saul, why are you persecuting Me?" (Acts 9:4 NKJV). Saul was struck blind. Jesus commanded Saul to go to Damascus and wait to be told what he must do. He was led to the city by those who were traveling with him and he waited for three days and nights without any food or water.

Ananias (not to be confused with Ananias the high priest or Ananias, Sapphira's husband, who lied to the Holy Spirit) was called "a disciple at Damascus." The Lord appeared to Ananias in a vision and told him, "Arise and go to the street called Straight and inquire at the house of Judas for one called Saul of Tarsus, for behold, he is praying" (Acts 9:11 NKJV).

Ananias responded to God's request: "Lord, I have heard from many about this man, how much harm he has done to Your saints in Jerusalem. And here he has authority from the chief priests to bind all who call on Your name" (Acts 9:13–14 NKJV).

Nevertheless, Ananias, probably shaking in his boots but still obedient, did what the Lord asked. Obedience is always better than sacrifice. And what a result! Something like scales fell from Saul's eyes and he could see again. What's more, it wasn't only his physical sight that was restored, but his spiritual sight as well. The falling scales were an outward sign of what was happing within Saul. Saul the persecutor become Paul the

Apostle, who went on to write thirteen books in the New Testament.

Paul's conversion experience is a pattern for all of us. First, Jesus must confront us with Himself, with our sin and rebellion against Him—even sins done in ignorance. Then we must humbly wait for His work to begin within us, work only He can do. Like Saul, God will find us—even when we are not looking for Him. He promises to fill us with His Spirit, so that we are equipped to do what He has called us to do!

Are you running on empty? Ask God, "Restore to me the joy of Your salvation..." (Psalm 51:12 NKJV). Ask Him for a fresh dose of His Holy Spirit! Ask God to help you "see" again, and overflow with the desire to obey the Lord in all you do.

Now get up and go into the city, and you will be told what you must do. — ***Acts 9:6 (NIV)***

CHAPTER NINE

It Ain't Over Till It's Over

If anyone sees his brother sinning a sin which does not lead to death, he will ask, and He will give him life for those who commit sin not leading to death. There is sin leading to death. I do not say that he should pray about that. — ***1 John 5:16 (NKJV)***

1 John 5:16 is a peculiar portion of Scripture. In it, God says believers are obligated to pray for a brother or sister who is in sin, but if that sin leads to death, then there is no obligation to pray for them.

Sometimes people slip away from the Lord. Maybe you are in that place right now. Perhaps you still come to church and sit through sermon after sermon, convicted of sin you are harboring in the depths of your heart—but you just aren't in a place to change and make things right.

The Bible speaks of people in whom, unfortunately, God was finished with. Korah, Dathan, and Abiram suffered what the Bible calls "sin leading to death" when their pride and ambition caused them to rebel against the priesthood of Aaron. They falsely accused Moses and Aaron of taking honor to themselves. For this sin, the ground under them split apart and swallowed them and their households, and all their possessions!

Nadab and Abihu continually disobeyed God, ultimately bringing "strange fire" as an offering to the Lord. Fire immediately came out from the presence of God and consumed them (Leviticus 10:1).

Ananias and Sapphira tried to deceive the Apostles and lied to the Holy Spirit—all in the name of the Lord. The Lord would not have it, and Acts 5:5 says "they fell down and died" (NIV). Now, we don't know how long God had been offering them grace and time to repent for their sin. All we know is that when God said enough was enough, they breathed their last breath.

You may not be in right standing with God. If this is true of you, you probably know it. Others likely know it too. However, with God it ain't over till it's over! You still have time to mend your relationship with your spouse, or restore a broken relationship with a child or sibling. You still have time to repent of hidden sin or even distance between a friend. And if you are reading this and have not accepted Jesus as your Lord and Savior, you still have time to accept this free gift of salvation and receive eternal life!

It isn't over till it's over. If you are reading this, you are still on this earth so there is still time. However, one day the Lord will decide your time on earth is finished. Don't be like Korah, Dathan, Abiram, Nadab, Abihu, Ananias, and Sapphira. Seek to restore your relationship with God and others so that one day, even after your death, you will continue to be a blessing to others, too.

> *So it was, as they were burying a man, that suddenly they spied a band of raiders; and they put the man in the tomb of Elisha; and when the man was let down and touched the bones of Elisha, he revived and stood on his feet.* — ***2 Kings 13:21 (NKJV)***

CHAPTER TEN

Watch Out for the Viper!

Now when they had escaped, they then found out that the island was called Malta. And the natives showed us unusual kindness; for they kindled a fire and made us all welcome, because of the rain that was falling and because of the cold. But when Paul had gathered a bundle of sticks and laid them on the fire, a viper came out because of the heat, and fastened on his hand. So when the natives saw the creature hanging from his hand, they said to one another, "No doubt this man is a murderer, whom, though he has escaped the sea, yet justice does not allow to live." But he shook off the creature into the fire and suffered no harm. However, they were expecting that he would swell up or suddenly fall down dead. But after they had looked for a long time and saw no harm come to him, they changed their minds and said that he was a god. — ***Acts 28:1–6 (NKJV)***

Paul had suffered numerous persecutions in his ministry work. Perhaps you, too, have been persecuted for the sake of the gospel. Paul had been falsely accused of *all* manner of things. His only "offense" was preaching the gospel of Christ! Some people had even vowed that they would not eat or drink until they had succeeded in killing Paul!

In Acts 28:1–7, Paul was ministering to the natives on the island of Malta when a viper slithered up and attached itself to Paul's hand. The natives were sure Paul would die! But Scripture says Paul shook off the viper into the campfire. Immediately, Paul's skeptics changed their minds.

We, too, must "shake the vipers off" into the fire.

Whenever anyone is seeking revival, there will always be a "viper" waiting to stop them from experiencing God's best. Vipers represent a demonic presence, opposition, or roadblocks. Satan did not want Paul to reach the natives of Malta or the people in Rome where he was headed next. Satan knew Paul's intention was to preach the gospel of Christ. So, Satan attacked Paul in the form of the viper with the intent to stop the spread of the gospel.

"Vipers" will show up in the lives of God's people in a number of ways. It may be in the form of various afflictions; certainly, Paul experienced his fair share! But the Bible says, "Many are the afflictions of the righteous, But the Lord delivers him out of them all" (Psalm 34:19 NKJV). Vipers may show up in the form of shame or disgrace, but God says, "Weeping may stay for the night, but rejoicing comes in the morning" (Psalm 30:5 NIV). Vipers may be man-given names that God did not bestow on His people (no good, worthless, unloved), an untimely death, or different types of bondage like fear of failure, poverty, or low self-esteem.

However, 1 John 4:4 says, "He who is in you is greater than he who is in the world" (NKJV). Christ in you can defeat any one of these "vipers." Like Paul, you need only to trust in the power of Christ and "shake off" any vipers that try to divert you from the purpose God has for you! Press on, and fight the good fight!

I have fought the good fight, I have finished the race, I have kept the faith. — ***2 Timothy 4:7 (NIV)***

CHAPTER ELEVEN

Take Off Your Shoes and Come On In!

Now Moses was tending the flock of Jethro his father-in-law, the priest of Midian. And he led the flock to the back of the desert, and came to Horeb, the mountain of God. 2 And the Angel of the Lord appeared to him in a flame of fire from the midst of a bush. So he looked, and behold, the bush was burning with fire, but the bush was not consumed. Then Moses said, "I will now turn aside and see this great sight, why the bush does not burn." So when the Lord saw that he turned aside to look, God called to him from the midst of the bush and said, "Moses, Moses!" And he said, "Here I am." Then He said, "Do not draw near this place. Take your sandals off your feet, for the place where you stand is holy ground." 6 Moreover He said, "I am the God of your father—the God of Abraham, the God of Isaac, and the God of Jacob." And Moses hid his face, for he was afraid to look upon God. — ***Exodus 3:1-6 (NKJV)***

The shoes in the Bible was more than just shoes. Shoes could indicate a person's social or financial status or show membership to a particular group. Removing the shoes meant a loss of dignity or the transfer of property.

The shoes was also not to be worn in certain places. Thus, the shoes were both a symbol of dignified dress while also being associated with dirt and dust—unfit for holy places and holy activity.

When God tells Moses and the priests to take their sandals off for "the place where you stand is holy ground," not one but both shoes were to be removed. The Greek word for 'holy' is *hagios*, which means to be separated or "set apart."[7] Biblically, when a person, place, or thing is "holy," it means it is separated from sin and consecrated for God for holy use. God was instructing Moses on the proper way to approach God in His holy dwelling place.

Is it the shoes that is unfit for a holy place? No, not exactly. The removal of a person's sandals signified removal of contaminants, such as before entering a house, but there is a much deeper lesson God is communicating by this act of obedience. When we approach God, we must approach Him as clean, holy, "set apart" vessels. Isaiah 59:2 says that "But your iniquities have separated you from your God; and your sins have hidden His face from you" (NKJV).

Because of this, we must be cleansed before entering the presence of God! Paul wrote to the Corinthian church about the necessity of being purified before God, saying, "Therefore, having these promises, beloved, let us cleanse ourselves from all filthiness of the flesh and spirit, perfecting holiness in the fear of God" (NKJV). It is to be done with humility and with reverence.

The church is the body of Christ, the temple of and witness to God. Worship, therefore, should be done out of a pure heart: "God is Spirit, and those who worship Him must worship in spirit and truth" (John 4:24 NKJV). Will you "take off your shoes," humbling yourself before God, repenting, and obeying His Word, in the knowledge that you are the temple of the Holy Spirit?

> *Who shall not fear You, O Lord, and glorify Your name? For You alone are holy.* — ***Revelation 15:4 (NKJV)***

CHAPTER TWELVE

The Role of the Prophet

By a prophet the LORD brought Israel out of Egypt, and by a prophet was he preserved. — ***Hosea 12:13 (NKJV)***

Hosea 12:13 reveals one of the primary functions of the prophet's ministry: preservation. God called Moses to deliver Israel from bondage in Egypt, and as such Moses interceded between God and Egypt as the nation's "preserver." (Numbers 14:11–20).

To "preserve" means to keep, save, or protect from harm, damage, loss, or decay.[8] In the original Hebrew of Hosea 12:13, the word used is *shamar*. *Shamar* means to watch, guard, protect, or tend to someone or something.[9] Essentially, it means to be a watchman, and biblically it maintains the protective element of the prophet's calling. The first time the word *shamar* is used in the Bible is in Genesis 2:15, when Adam was told to keep (*shamar*) the garden.[10] It can refer to guarding a flock, the heart, the mind, a nation, or a city from outside attacks or ungodly influences. It is a word that is used to describe keeping (guarding) the gates or entries to cities.

Today, churches desperately need this preserving and guarding aspect of the prophet's ministry! Notice what God says in the Bible about the importance of the watchman's (*shamar*) role:

> *Unless the LORD builds the house, they labor in vain who build it; unless the LORD guards the city, the watchman stays awake in vain.* — ***Psalm 127:1 (NKJV)***

> *My soul waits for the Lord more than those who watch for the morning—yes, more than those who watch for the morning.* — ***Psalm 130:6 (NKJV)***

> *I have set watchmen on your walls, O Jerusalem; They shall never hold their peace day or night. You who make mention of the LORD, do not keep silent* — ***Isaiah 62:6 (NKJV)***

How is this unique role of the prophet accomplished? Though intercession, discernment, praise, preaching, teaching, and worship. God is the ultimate *shamar* of His people, watching over them and keeping guard against evil. He watches over His people: "He who keeps Israel shall never slumber or sleep" (Psalm 121:4 NKJV). He also guards our minds and our hearts: "And the peace of God, which surpasses all understanding, will guard your hearts and minds through Christ Jesus" (Philippians 4:7 NKJV). This is God's very nature, and as His representatives on earth, we are to do the same for our brothers and sisters. We are to keep watch and to guard. We are to take up this responsibility, and help defend God's church—the bride of Christ—against error, division, legalism, and deception in these last days.

Typically, pastors are identified as the spiritual guardians of the church, overlooking the role of the prophet. However, the church was never intended to function only with pastors, but many different roles—apostles, prophets, teachers, and miracle workers (1 Corinthians 12:29). There is a specific role for the prophet, designed to be the foundation of God's household.

Has God's still, small voice been speaking to you? How might you be gifted, in accordance with keeping God's household in order?

> *Now, therefore, you are no longer strangers and foreigners, but fellow citizens with the saints and members of the household of God, having been built on the foundation of the apostles and prophets, Jesus Christ Himself being the chief cornerstone, in whom the whole building, being fitted together, grows into a holy temple in the Lord* — ***Ephesians 2:19–21(NKJV)***

CHAPTER THIRTEEN

My "-ites" Are About to Take Flight

So Joshua said to the children of Israel, "Come here, and hear the words of the LORD your God." And Joshua said, "By this you shall know that the living God is among you, and that He will without fail drive out from before you the Canaanites and the Hittites and the Hivites and the Perizzites and the Girgashites and the Amorites and the Jebusites." — ***Joshua 3:9–10 (NKJV)***

God reassured Joshua before crossing the Jordan River into the Promised Land that even though there were more powerful enemy nations waiting, He would be with them. These "-ite" nations—the Canaanites, Hittites, Hivites, Perizzites, Girgashites, Amorites, and Jebusites—were seven nations "greater and stronger than you..." (Deuteronomy 7:1 NASB).

Yet in Deuteronomy 7:1, God also had promised Israel He would "clear away many nations before you" (NASB). The battle ahead had already been won before it started! However, Israel still had to go and fight the enemy that stood in the way of Israel's promise being fulfilled.

Similarly, we are in a battle that we must fight, but it is not against flesh and blood:

> *For we do not wrestle against flesh and blood, but against principalities, against powers, against the rulers of the darkness of this age, against spiritual hosts of wickedness in the heavenly places. —* ***Ephesians 6:12 (NKJV)***

Our battle is against the demonic powers that stand in the way of our promises being realized. But God is able, present and willing to help us overcome those problems that are "greater and stronger" than we. Though there is a very real enemy who will try everything in his limited power to defeat us, it's important to remember God will take care of all the "–ites" in our life. They will take flight!

Each of these nations had certain characteristics. Consider what these "–ites" are for New Testament believers:[11]

- Hittites — subliminal torments, phobias, terror, depression, deceit
- Girgashites — focus on earthliness, unbelief in what cannot be seen
- Amorites — obsession with earthly fame and glory, domineering
- Canaanites — addictions, perversions, exaggerated people-pleasing

- Perizzites — limited vision, laziness, low self-esteem
- Hivites — vision limited to enjoying an earthly inheritance, hedonism
- Jebusites — suppression of spiritual authority in fellow believers, legalism

There is no enemy that has any authority to render us fearful, weak, or feeble. No "–ites" should be holding on to our blessings. No "–ites" should be possessing our land, homes, jobs, churches, healings, or inheritance. That promise was guaranteed through an unconditional covenant God made with Abraham which said, "I am the LORD, who brought you out of Ur of the Chaldeans, to give you this land to inherit it" (Genesis 15:7 NKJV). Thousands of years later, Paul wrote to the Gentile Galatian church "that the blessing of Abraham might come upon the Gentiles in Christ Jesus, that we might receive the promise of the Spirit through faith" (Galatians 3:14 NKJV).

The promise of an inheritance, a "good land of rest" where all enemies are defeated, is waiting for anyone who puts their trust in Jesus through faith! Have you trusted Him? If so, trust in God who promises to "clear away many nations before you!" (Deuteronomy 7:1 NASB). Your "–ites" are about to take flight!

The Lord will cause your enemies who rise against you to be defeated before your face; they shall come out against you one way and flee before you seven ways.
— Deuteronomy 28:7 (NKJV)

CHAPTER FOURTEEN

Hard Lessons from a King

And he built fortified cities in Judah, for the land had rest; he had no war in those years, because the LORD had given him rest. Therefore he said to Judah, "Let us build these cities and make walls around them, and towers, gates, and bars, while the land is yet before us, because we have sought the LORD our God; we have sought Him, and He has given us rest on every side." So they built and prospered. And Asa had an army of three hundred thousand from Judah who carried shields and spears, and from Benjamin two hundred and eighty thousand men who carried shields and drew bows; all these were mighty men of valor. — ***2 Chronicles 14:6–8 (NKJV)***

Asa, a king of Judah whose name means "physician" or "healer," was the son of Abijah and grandson of Rehoboam. Asa was among the few kings of Judah (and Israel) who was faithful to God—at least at the beginning of his reign (912—872 BC). Asa vigorously opposed idolatry, along with the immoral behavior that accompanied it.

Initially, Asa's dislike for idolatry was remarkable, and his obedience to God was equally remarkable. God gave him specific orders to build. So, Asa told the Israelites:

> *Let us build these cities and make walls around them, and towers, gates, and bars, while the land is yet before us, because we have sought the LORD our God; we have sought Him, and He has given us rest on every side.* — ***2 Chronicles 14:7 (NKJV)***

Asa stepped out of the way and followed God's direction. For his obedience God rewarded him and his kingdom with security and prosperity. However, something happened in the thirty-fifth year of his reign that changed this.

Baasha, the king of Israel, blocked Judah's trade routes. Typically, this was an indication that an invasion was close behind. Instead of seeking the Lord's direction and strength, Asa stole silver and gold from the temple treasury to bribe Baasha. This angered God, who said:

> *For the eyes of the LORD run to and fro throughout the whole earth, to show Himself strong on behalf of those whose heart is loyal to Him. In this you have done foolishly; therefore from now on you shall have wars.*
> ***— 2 Chronicles 16:9 (NKJV)***

Asa's heart was divided, and the consequence was severe: his nation would face continual war.

In the thirty-ninth year of his reign, Asa became seriously ill with a severe disease of his feet. Instead of trusting God, he trusted only in the man—in human doctors. Somewhere during his reign, Asa had slipped into what is called "secular humanism," the belief that man is capable of morality and self-fulfillment absent of God.

Paul wrote to the Romans, "Whatever was written in former days was written for our instruction, so that by steadfastness and by the encouragement of the scriptures we might have hope" (Romans 15:4 NRSV). There is much to learn from Asa's mistakes! It is foolish to trust man over God, who is all-seeing and all-knowing. We must step aside, and let God have His way—for it is a superior way!

Trust in the LORD with all your heart, And lean not on your own understanding; In all your ways acknowledge Him, And He shall direct your paths. — ***Proverbs 3:5–6 (NKJV)***

CHAPTER FIFTEEN

Break Away, Put Away, and Stay Away

Jehoshaphat had riches and honor in abundance; and by marriage he allied himself with Ahab. After some years he went down to visit Ahab in Samaria; and Ahab killed sheep and oxen in abundance for him and the people who were with him, and persuaded him to go up with him to Ramoth Gilead. So Ahab king of Israel said to Jehoshaphat king of Judah, "Will you go with me against Ramoth Gilead?" And he answered him, "I am as you are, and my people as your people; we will be with you in the war." Also Jehoshaphat said to the king of Israel, "Please inquire for the word of the Lord today." Then the king of Israel gathered the prophets together, four hundred men, and said to them, "Shall we go to war against Ramoth Gilead, or shall I refrain?" So they said, "Go up, for God will deliver it into the king's hand." — **2 Chronicles 18:1–5 (NKJV)**

An ice cream Sunday may seem decadent—unless you are allergic to dairy, in which case choosing to partake will likely result in a very upset stomach! Sometimes something may look good, sound good, and even taste good but not be good for you.

King Jehoshaphat, king of Judah, experienced abundant prosperity as a result of obeying God. King Ahab, a very powerful king of Israel who was evil to the core, experienced the *image* of abundance. To people standing on the outside, his reign "looked good." In reality, Ahab was in debt, broke, and evil. However, Ahab deceived the king of Judah by inviting him to his house for a feast. He served Jehoshaphat and his entire caravan fresh lamb and oxtails (a delicacy in that day). Ahab was a complete counterfeit! But this phony image tricked Jehoshaphat.

Scripture indicates Jehoshaphat had wealth and honor, so there was no apparent reason for him even to dabble with a relationship with Ahab. Judah was already a nation experiencing peace. Jehoshaphat had received an abundant blessing from God, and God certainly did not tell Jehoshaphat to seek out an alliance with Ahab.

Jehoshaphat had no previous dealings with Ahab. Before he knew it, however, Jehoshaphat had hastily agreed to go to battle with Ahab and could not back out. Ahab even boasted four hundred fake prophets for spiritual guidance—further deceiving Jehoshaphat. The alliance "looked" good, but was something Jehoshaphat should never have fallen for.

A demonic deception that tugged on Jehoshaphat's heart strings caused him to fall for this Jezebel-derived plan. Jehoshaphat began to feel an affinity for Ahab—a spontaneous sympathy or liking for him.

It was this demon of sympathy that led Jehoshaphat into this ungodly alliance. For modern-day believers, this demonic influence can be just as powerful. You may find yourself saying, "I don't know what came over me. I just felt like…" or "I've never done this before but I feel led to…." When this happens, it is critical to break away, put away, and stay away from what or who might be deceiving you.

Jehoshaphat's mistake was forming a partnership with a man who rejected the Lord. He followed the popular religion of the day, first with Ahab, then Ahaziah, and then Jehoram—and God was not pleased. In the same way, believers are not to form modern-day partnerships with the world! James 4:4 says, "Do you not know that friendship with the world is enmity with God? Whoever therefore wants to be a friend of the world makes himself an enemy of God" (NKJV).

Instead, break away (separate or detach), stay away (keep one's distance from), and put away (renounce or discard) anything that might deceive you into thinking something is of God when it is not. If you have a friendship with a person who does not love God that may be destructive, break it off. If there is an addictive substance you are repeatedly drawn to, stay away from anything that would tempt you to use it. Finally, renounce anything in your life that is not of God.

> *Therefore, brethren, be even more diligent to make your call and election sure, for if you do these things you will never stumble; for so an entrance will be supplied to you abundantly into the everlasting kingdom of our Lord and Savior Jesus Christ.* — ***2 Peter 1:10–11 (NKJV)***

CHAPTER SIXTEEN

Keep the Main Thing as the Main Thing

We can make our plans, but the LORD determines our steps.
— Proverbs 16:9 (NLT)

There is nothing like changes in one's travel plans to reveal how we truly can handle change. Some people love to research through Travelocity, Expedia, and many other sites to solidify the best deal for a vacation trip. They plan for months ahead, book the best flights, and reserve the perfect hotel to accommodate their stay. They may even research the best restaurants and shopping centers. However, one delayed flight, unforeseen storm or bad hotel experience can ruin an entire trip.

Changes for most people equals stress, hassles, and more work. But sometimes God changes plans to reveal something a person couldn't see prior, or He changes plans because they're not *His* plans. God already has a plan for your life—including every minute detail—and it is good! "For I know the thoughts that I think toward you, says the LORD, thoughts of peace and not of evil, to give you a future and a hope" (Jeremiah 29:11 NKJV).

Even though we might know this, it is human nature to try and take control of life and make God's plans for Him. There is a common saying: "If you want to make God laugh, tell him your plans!" God is certainly not malicious in His laughter—but He probably chuckles at how human beings think they have any right to determine the course of their life in the first place.

Recognize the plans you make may seem right to you, but may be selfish at the root and potentially lead to negative results. Proverbs 16:25 says, "There is a way that seems right to a man, but its end is the way of death" (NKJV). The good news is God is in the business of altering mankind's plans to His plan—and His plan brings *life*! Jesus came that God's children "may have life, and that they may have it more abundantly" (John 10:10 NKJV).

One of Jesus' disciples, Peter, became extremely upset at Jesus when He talked about his impending death. "Far be it from You, Lord; this shall not happen to You!" (Matthew 16:22 NKJV) he declared. "That's not my plan," Peter was probably thinking. Then Jesus rebuked him, saying, "Get behind Me, Satan! You are an offense to Me, for you are not mindful of the things of God, but the things of men" (Matthew 16:23 NKJV).

Peter's plans were just that—they were his plans. He could not see that God's plan involving Jesus' death also included His resurrection and ascension—and ultimately the redemption of the entire world! To best deal with shifts in our plans, we must keep God's thoughts in the forefront of our mind. Jesus told His disciples:

> *If anyone desires to come after Me, let him deny himself, and take up his cross, and follow Me. For whoever desires to save his life will lose it, but whoever loses his life for My sake will find it.* — ***Matthew 16:24–25 (NKJV)***

Following Jesus will require a change in your plans. Relinquish or (deny) your desire to plan, scheme, and insist on your way; instead, surrender your daily life to Jesus.

God's plans are good, and they will result in something much better than you and I could ever hope for!

> *Now to Him who is able to do exceedingly abundantly above all that we ask or think, according to the power that works in us.* — ***Ephesians 3:20 (NKJV)***

CHAPTER SEVENTEEN

Don't Let Fear Control Your Life

For God has not given us a spirit of fear, but of power and of love and of a sound mind. — ***2 Timothy 1:7 (NKJV)***

Fear will control a person's life; it affects what a person hears others say and sees others do. It is an attitude that can change the meaning of words and gestures others use when speaking. Fear devalues a person, and causes them to think people are "always putting me down."

Fear is also the biggest enemy of faith. Fear has many appearances, but the foundation of most of what people call fear is vanity and insecurity, or the habit of accepting a lie rather than the truth. It manifests in the fear of looking foolish, being rejected, being wrong, not pleasing men, not being good enough, or failing.

David had every reason to be fearful! Saul, raging with jealousy, attempted to kill him and persecuted him relentlessly. David had to fight a Philistine giant with nothing but a few smooth stones. Later as king, David's own sons connived and conspired to take control of the kingdom and threatened their own father's life—just as Saul had done!

However, David is never characterized in Scripture as being fearful; in fact, he is described as being a man after God's own heart (Acts 13:22). Why? Because of his faith in God. Notice what David cries out in Psalm 141:

> *But my eyes are upon You, O GOD the Lord; in You I take refuge; do not leave my soul destitute. Keep me from the snares they have laid for me, and from the traps of the workers of iniquity. Let the wicked fall into their own nets, while I escape safely.* — ***Psalm 141:8–10 (NKJV)***

Instead of fearing his enemies, David kept his eyes on God. In the midst of persecution, David thanked and praised God saying, "You are great, O LORD GOD. For there is none like You, nor is there any God besides You, according to *all that we have heard with our ears*" (2 Samuel 7:22 NKJV, emphasis added). The Bible says that God "has not given us a spirit of fear, but of power and of love and of a sound mind" (2 Timothy 1:7 NKJV) and that God's people should "not in any way [be] terrified by your adversaries" (Philippians 1:28 NKJV).

What then is the key to breaking fear? It is faith in God and love. The writer of Hebrews said, "Now faith is the substance of things hoped for, the evidence of things not seen" (Hebrews 11:1 NKJV) and 1 John 4:18 says, "There is no fear in love; but perfect love casts out fear, because fear involves torment. But he who fears has not been made perfect in love" (NKJV). Child of God, you do not have a spirit of fear, but one of power and love!

Living without fear can only happen in Christ. Fearlessness does not deny the presence of fear; rather, it is a place of position and power that breeds confidence and assurance.

John Newton once wrote:

> If the Lord be with us, we have no cause of fear. His eye is upon us, His arm over us, His ear open to our prayer—His grace sufficient, His promise unchangeable.[12]

Ultimately, fear will hold you back and prevent you from being what God calls you to be. What lie is causing you to fear? The Lord is your cheerleader (Psalm 118:6), and He will never leave you or forsake you (Hebrews 13:5). You have nothing to fear!

> *The LORD is my light and my salvation; Whom shall I fear? The LORD is the strength of my life; Of whom shall I be afraid?* — ***Psalm 27:1 (NKJV)***

CHAPTER EIGHTEEN

Rooted in God's Presence

The righteous shall flourish like a palm tree, He shall grow like a cedar in Lebanon. Those who are planted in the house of the LORD Shall flourish in the courts of our God. They shall still bear fruit in old age; They shall be fresh and flourishing. — ***Psalm 92:12–14 (NKJV)***

Farmers have a great responsibility. They prepare the soil, plant seeds at the right time, water the seeds, fertilize when necessary, and watch over their garden to ensure an abundant harvest. In the Bible, believers are often compared to plants. Isaiah 61:3 calls those who trust in God "trees of righteous, the planting of the LORD, that He may be glorified" (NKJV).

The gardener's responsibility is to enable a plant to grow and mature. God, as the Master Gardener, has "planted" believers in Christ. He waters those who have put their faith in Jesus with the Living Water of the Holy Spirit and the presence of the Lord and fertilizes with spiritual discipline and accountability.

Paul wrote that God's righteousness is poured out to believers through faith in Jesus Christ, "to all and on all who believe" (Romans 3:22 NKJV). And Psalm 92 says, "The righteous shall flourish…" (Psalm 92:12 NKJV). They will break forth, bud and bloom, spread and prosper. They will also be "fresh and flourishing…" (Psalm 92:14 NKJV). Some Bibles translate 'fresh' as 'fat.' This word comes from the Hebrew word *dashen*, which means to be, grow, or become fat or prosperous, or to be anointed.[13]

The results are "plants," or believers, that are so satisfied and anointed by God they naturally produce much fruit:

> *But the fruit of the Spirit is love, joy, peace, longsuffering, kindness, goodness, faithfulness, gentleness, self-control. Against such there is no law.* — ***Galatians 5:22–23 (NKJV)***

God's very character is reproduced and multiplied in believers. However, there is a key for this flourishing to happen. Those who produce fruit are those who are planted in the house of the Lord. This is more garden imagery, since "to plant" means "to put down roots" (Psalm 92:14).

To be "planted in the house of the LORD" (Psalm 92:13 NKJV) means to be planted in the courts of God—His dwelling place, or in His presence. Psalm 84:10 says, "For a day in Your courts is better than a thousand. I would rather be a doorkeeper in the house of my God Than dwell in the tents of wickedness" (Psalm 84:10

NKJV). A day in God's presence is better than a thousand without! This is what satisfies the soul.

This spiritual principle of gardening goes back to the garden of Eden. Genesis 2:8 says, "The LORD God planted a garden eastward in Eden, and there He put the man whom He had formed" (Genesis 2:8 NKJV). God then immediately commanded the people he created to multiply. From the beginning of time, God is seen as a gardener—preparing, planting, fertilizing, and ultimately harvesting a people for Himself.

God is watching over you, His tender "plant." He will do whatever is necessary to ensure you grow and mature according to His plan, even if it means a time of fertilizing or discipline. You are part of a great harvest of believers that the Master Gardener is tending! But to grow, you must remain in His presence—planted in His house.

Put in the sickle, for the harvest is ripe. — ***Joel 3:13 (NKJV)***

CHAPTER NINETEEN

Broken-Up Ground

Break up your fallow ground, and do not sow among thorns. — ***Jeremiah 4:3 (NKJV)***

Sow for yourselves righteousness, reap the fruit of unfailing love, and break up your unplowed ground; for it is time to seek the LORD, until he comes and showers righteousness on you. — ***Hosea 10:12 (NIV)***

These two passages in Jeremiah and Hosea have in common the phrase, "Break up your unplowed (fallow) ground." Just what does this mean?

Breaking up fallow ground indicates the believer's responsibility in tending to their walk with Christ. The phrase "unplowed ground" (Hosea 10:12 NIV) or "fallow ground" is the Hebrew noun *nîr*, which means "the tillable, untilled, or fallow ground."[14] It is land that could be fruitful, but for whatever reason has not been broken up, cultivated, farmed, and primed for planting.

The prophets commanded the people to take apart the literal land. Fallow ground is both unusable and unused.

Unplowed ground is unusable because crops simply cannot grow. Seeds cannot penetrate hard soil; they will not germinate and grow into maturity. Jeremiah said that because the people didn't bother to prepare the soil and pull out thorns, the seed did not produce! There is a deeply profound spiritual lesson here. Has your heart been hardened with hatred or bitterness? Have you struggled with lust, greed or covetousness? These things must be broken up, as a plow does the hard work of opening up the ground.

Is there unbelief lurking in your soul? Has someone hurt you so deeply you have sealed off an area of your life to suppress the pain? Allow God to plow the hardness of your soul and heal your hurts. He will do the difficult work if you will let Him! That hardness of unbelief must be faced and broken up if God is to start something new and fruitful in your heart. Confessing and repenting is one way to dig deep and break up hard heart-soil. When is the last time you prostrated yourself before the Lord, broken and ready to be used?

Finally, thorns must be collected and incinerated. When a field goes unplanted for numerous years, it often becomes covered with thorns or other weeds. What kinds of thistles may be making the areas (fields) of your heart unproductive? In the Parable of the Sower, Jesus used thorns in a field to describe the human heart:

> *Now he who received seed among the thorns is he who hears the word, and the cares of this world and the*

deceitfulness of riches choke the word, and he becomes unfruitful" — ***Matthew 13:22 (NKJV)***

Break up the hard soil in your life, so that what was once unusable will become a rich soil that God can use to bear much fruit for the kingdom!

It was planted in good soil by many waters, To bring forth branches, bear fruit, And become a majestic vine.
— ***Ezekiel 17:8 (NKJV)***

CHAPTER TWENTY

Angels Among Us

Behold, I send an Angel before you to keep you in the way and to bring you into the place which I have prepared. Beware of Him and obey His voice; do not provoke Him, for He will not pardon your transgressions; for My name is in Him. — ***Exodus 23:20–21 (NKJV)***

Many people seem to have a keen interest—if not an obsession—in angels, but often don't have a *biblical* understanding. Their image of angels come from movies and books and pictures created by man. In fact, there is an actual word to describe the obsession the word has with angels: *angelmania*![15]

However, God, not Newsweek, is the ultimate revealer of truth regarding angels, and He was not quiet on the subject—in fact, the Bible tells us quite a bit about these supernatural beings. The word 'angel' comes from the Greek word *aggelos*, which means "messenger"[16] in the New Testament. The Hebrew word used is *mal'ak*, and it too means "messenger."[17]

Hebrews 12:22 mentions a countless "company of angels" (Hebrews 12:22 NKJV) while John wrote in Revelation, "Then I looked, and I heard the voice of many angels around the throne, the living creatures, and the elders; and the number of them was ten thousand times ten thousand, and thousands of thousands" (Revelation 5:11 NKJV) circling God's throne.

Angels don't marry, and they don't die, according to Luke 20:35–36. Zechariah said that they bring messages to God's people (Zechariah 1:14–17). They praise God (Revelation 5:11–12) and protect His people (Daniel 6:22). Angels are ministering spirits, as seen in how angels cared for Jesus after He prayed in the garden of Gethsemane (Luke 22:38–43). Angels led Moses into the Promised Land (Exodus 23:20), so we know they direct people. Some angels have wings, like seraphim (Isaiah 6:2, 6:6), but most do not. And the Bible tells us their principle job is to praise and worship the King! (Isaiah 6:3).

Most often people associate angels as being good, but 2 Peter 2:4 tells us you can't trust every angel. Some angels, known as "fallen angels," rebelled against God. The chief fallen angel is Satan, whose main goal is to draw believers away from God and to tempt people into sin (Romans 8:38–39; 1 Peter 5:8). And Scripture is very clear that there was an angelic conflict in heaven where a company of angels lead by the Archangel Michael—the chief prince—fought and kicked Satan and his followers out of heaven! (Revelation 12:7-9)

In spite of this, the Bible teaches more about angels by what it *doesn't* say. Scripture never teaches us to study angels or look for their appearance. Though Hebrews 13:2 says you and I may have even entertained angels without realizing it, we are never told to watch for them.

Instead, we are to look "unto Jesus, the author and finisher of our faith, who for the joy that was set before Him endured the cross, despising the shame, and has sat down at the right hand of the throne of God" (Hebrews 12:2 NKJV). Tony Evans writes in his book *The Truth about Angels and Demons*:

> As created beings, angels are not to be worshipped, glorified, or adored in and of themselves. The angels were created to worship, glorify, adore, and obey God.[18]

Therefore, focus on God, and worship Him alone.

> *I have set the LORD always before me; because He is at my right hand I shall not be moved.* — ***Psalm 16:8 (NKJV)***

CHAPTER TWENTY-ONE

No Pain, No Gain!

And lest I should be exalted above measure by the abundance of the revelations, a thorn in the flesh was given to me, a messenger of Satan to buffet me, lest I be exalted above measure. Concerning this thing I pleaded with the Lord three times that it might depart from me. And He said to me, "My grace is sufficient for you, for My strength is made perfect in weakness." Therefore most gladly I will rather boast in my infirmities, that the power of Christ may rest upon me. Therefore I take pleasure in infirmities, in reproaches, in needs, in persecutions, in distresses, for Christ's sake. For when I am weak, then I am strong.
— 2 Corinthians 12:7–10 (KJV)

In Greek, the word for 'thorn' is the word *skolops*, which means "something which frustrates and causes trouble in the lives of those afflicted."[19] Paul described some kind of thorn in his life, but recognized it as a gift that kept him from becoming conceited. Theologians differ on what the thorn might be, in a physical sense; the most widely accepted explanation is that it was a chronic condition of poor vision (ophthalmia).[20]

But then Paul said that this thorn was a messenger of Satan to "buffet" him. The word 'buffet' means "to drive, force, move, or attack by or as if by repeated blows."[21] Whatever (or whoever) it was that Paul endured, he compared it to being beaten. In spite of this, Paul knew that the pain he was undergoing would eventually bring about God's good—*no pain, no gain!*

Sometimes it may feel like you are experiencing an unfair or unendurable amount of pain, a "thorn" of sorts. However, remember what Paul was able to say: God's grace was enough, and in Paul's weakness God's strength was revealed. Rest assured; everyone will go through some sort of pain in this life; though it might look like others are carefree with no troubles, if you are human you will eventually experience pain, hurt, financial stress, or illness. Jesus affirmed this in John 6:33 when He said, "In the world you will have tribulation; but be of good cheer, I have overcome the world" (NKJV).

Paul's thorn was "in the flesh." It afflicted his physical man. Often, the thorns and buffetings we experience in this life display themselves in the physical realm, through ailments and other forms of physical suffering. At other times, it will surface in emotional pain, such as depression, loneliness, and heartbreak. Sometimes thorns will be spiritual in nature, such as unbelief or pride. Still, God allows for these thorns; though it may not make sense at the moment, God sees what we cannot yet see.

The word 'buffet' is a verb written in the present tense, active voice. This means the action is continual in nature. In other words, Paul lived with this thing all the time! Sometimes an illness or a hurt is temporary; but sometimes, the "thorn" never goes away. Be encouraged! Jesus knows what it means to suffer; one day, however, God will make all things knew and those who trust in Jesus in spite of suffering and pain will be renewed and glorified with Jesus!

> *The Spirit Himself bears witness with our spirit that we are children of God, and if children, then heirs—heirs of God and joint heirs with Christ, if indeed we suffer with Him, that we may also be glorified together.* ***—Romans 8:16–18 (NKJV)***

CHAPTER TWENTY-TWO

A Plan above All Plans

For I know the thoughts that I think toward you, says the LORD, thoughts of peace and not of evil, to give you a future and a hope. ***—Jeremiah 29:11 (NKJV)***

Some people are planners. They are "maximizers," making use of every minute of every day. Others like to fly by the seat of their pants—they have no plans and no goals. God is the ultimate maximizer—His plans are beyond even the best man-made plans! In fact, His plans are eternal and they involve the restoration of all things. His plans are above all plans.

We can see this plan enacted out in God's decision to choose (predestine) us before the foundation of the world "to be conformed to the image of His Son…" (Romans 8:29 NKJV). What a plan! God's plan from the inception of time was that sinful man would be conformed to be like Him.

The key to Paul's happiness and satisfaction was that he had a gratifying understanding that his days were governed by God's will. He knew God's plans were greater than his own. In 2 Thessalonians 2:13–15 Paul tells us:

> *But we ought always to thank God for you, brothers loved by the Lord, because from the beginning God chose you to be saved through the sanctifying work of the Spirit and through belief in the truth. He called you to this through our gospel, that you might share in the glory of our Lord Jesus Christ. So then, brothers, stand firm and hold to the teachings we passed on to you, whether by word of mouth or by letter.* ***(NIV)***

God's plan is set, but to be a part of this predetermined plan each person must choose to live within the will of God. God has a plan—*now you must decide to be a part of it.*

Not only were we predestined to be conformed into his image, but we were chosen to be holy and blameless, and adopted as his sons:

> *Praise be to the God and Father of our Lord Jesus Christ, who has blessed us in the heavenly realms with every spiritual blessing in Christ. For he chose us in him before the creation of the world to be holy and blameless in his sight. In love he predestined us to be adopted as his sons through Jesus Christ, in accordance with his pleasure and will-to the praise of his glorious grace, which he has freely given us in the One he loves. In him we have redemption through his blood, the forgiveness of sins, in accordance with the riches of God's grace that he lavished on us with all wisdom and understanding."* — ***Ephesians 1:3–8 (NIV)***

God who sees the end from the beginning knows how everything will work out. However, we can only see the here and now, and what has already happened. Sometimes it becomes hard for people to enjoy the blessing of living within the will of God because it seems restrictive. However, this is because we cannot see what is ahead and how it actually enlarges our life! Jesus promises this, telling his disciples that those who take up their cross and follow Him, those who lose their life for Him "will find it..." (Matthew 16:24 NIV). God has a plan above all plans. It is a beautiful plan, and it is eternal.

Great is our Lord, and mighty in power; His understanding is infinite. — ***Psalm 147:5 (NIV)***

CHAPTER TWENTY-THREE

On Eagles' Wings

But those who wait on the LORD shall renew their strength; they shall mount up with wings like eagles, they shall run and not be weary, they shall walk and not faint. — ***Isaiah 40:31 (NKJV)***

Think of an eagle, soaring high about the ground, making its nest in the cleft of massive rocks. Eagles are kings of the sky. With keenness of eye, they spy prey, swoop down to earth with tremendous speed, and with sharp, strong talons, snatch up its meal and soar to its nest to feast.

For centuries, eagles have been recognized by nations, kingdoms, and empires as the king of the birds. It is a symbol of power; people have connected eagles to the divine since they fly higher than any other bird! As such, nations have reproduced the eagle on coins, seals, emblems, and flags.

It's not surprising that this image runs throughout the pages of Scripture, too. Consider the following Scriptures, and how God is described like an eagle:

> *He rode upon a cherub, and flew; and He sped upon the wings of the wind* — ***Psalm 18:10 (NASB)***

> *You yourselves have seen what I did to the Egyptians, and how I bore you on eagles' wings and brought you to myself.* — ***Exodus 19:4 (NASB)***

> *Like an eagle that stirs up its nest, that hovers over its young, He spread His wings and caught them, He carried them on His pinions"* — ***Deuteronomy 32:11 (NASB)***

The eagle can bear up (carry) its young eaglets on its pinions, which are the outer wings. God carried Israel out of captivity from Egypt and continued to bear her up in her wanderings in the wilderness. But the majestic eagle is also a protector of its young. David draws on this imagery in Psalm 91:4, saying, "He shall cover you with His feathers, and under His wings you shall take refuge; His truth shall be your shield and buckler" (NKJV).

Moreover, just as the natural eaglets depend and live on the nourishment received from the parent eagle, believers should depend on and live on heavenly food—the Word of God. Picture a nest of baby eagles; the mother comes back with food, and what do the eaglets do? They open their mouths wide, waiting for her to drop the food in.

Is this how we approach God's Word? Mouths open wide, anticipating the "bread of life" that He wants to give His children? Matthew 4:4 says, "It is written, 'Man shall not live by bread alone, but by every word that proceeds from the mouth of God'" (NKJV).

God is powerful like an eagle. He covers His children, shadows them (Psalm 36:7, 63:7, 91:1–4, 1 Kings 8:7), hides them (Psalm 17:8), bears them up (Psalm 36:7), and feeds them. What an amazing picture of power and protection!

> *They shall mount up with wings like eagles, they shall run and not be weary, they shall walk and not faint.* — ***Isaiah 40:31 (NKJV)***

CHAPTER TWENTY-FOUR

Where Are the Spiritual Blacksmiths?

Now there was no blacksmith to be found throughout all the land of Israel, for the Philistines said, "Lest the Hebrews make swords or spears." — ***1 Samuel 13:19 (NKJV)***

Jonathan, a talented military leader, had gone ahead of his father and attacked the Philistines at Geba. It was an unauthorized attack that caused the Philistines to surround Israel with thousands of soldiers equipped with swords and chariots, intending to crush the Hebrews. The Israelites were terrified and hid wherever they could—in rocks, holes, and caves.

Then Samuel the prophet told Saul to wait for him to come to offer up the burnt offering. But Saul was impatient and took it upon himself to offer sacrifices. God responded by removing His hand from Saul, and thus from all of Israel. Saul's impatience had dramatic consequences. He tried to explain to Samuel why he did what he did, but Samuel reproved Saul for disobeying God telling Him his kingdom would come to an end. The Philistines indeed came out to squash Israel, and this is where 1 Samuel 19 gives a crucial piece of information: *there were no blacksmiths left in all of Israel!* There was no one left to make new weapons, and therefore Israel was an open target.

The Philistines had stripped Israel of her blacksmiths, leaving them empty-handed and without the best weapons. But likewise, Satan has stripped the church of its weapon-makers! *Spiritual* blacksmiths know how to flow in the anointing and break the yoke. They know how to move in spiritual authority, and how to move in the gifts of the Holy Spirit by walking in faith to cast out devils and flow in an apostolic, prophetic anointing. This generation is sorely lacking in spiritual blacksmiths, who make weapons to fight.

God declares how important it is to be ready for war, by preparing to fight the spiritual battles ahead:

> *Fight the good fight of faith, lay hold on eternal life, to which you were also called and have confessed the good confession in the presence of many witnesses.* — ***1 Timothy 6:12 (NKJV)***

> *Put on the whole armor of God, that you may be able to stand against the wiles of the devil.* — ***Ephesians 6:11 (NKJV)***

For the weapons of our warfare are not carnal but mighty in God for pulling down strongholds. — ***2 Corinthians 10:4 (NKJV)***

The Bible speaks of a time coming where we will "beat their swords into plowshares" (Isaiah 2:4 NKJV)—when we will not need weapons because Satan and his demons will be crushed. But this is not that time. This is a time for war, and the believer must be ready!

Sit under anointed blacksmiths who preach, pray, prophesy, and teach. This will sharpen you for ministry and prepare you for the battle not against flesh and blood, "but against principalities, against powers, against the rulers of the darkness of this age, against spiritual hosts of wickedness in the heavenly places" (Ephesians 6:12 NKJV).

CHAPTER TWENTY-FIVE

Do You Want to Be Made Well?

When Jesus saw him lying there, and knew that he already had been in that condition a long time, He said to him, "Do you want to be made well?" The sick man answered Him, "Sir, I have no man to put me into the pool when the water is stirred up; but while I am coming, another steps down before me." Jesus said to him, "Rise, take up your bed and walk." And immediately the man was made well, took up his bed, and walked. ***— John 5:6–8 (NKJV)***

In ancient Jerusalem, by the sheep's gate, there was a pool of water called Bethesda. Five covered colonnades encircled the pool, which was associated with healing. Multitudes of sick, blind, lame, and paralyzed people waited daily for the stirring of the water by the angel of the Lord; the first person who stepped into the pool after the water was stirred would be healed from their infirmity.

A certain man had been sick for thirty-eight years. This man would lie near the pool every day hoping this would be his time of healing. On this day, Jesus showed up and discerned the man's handicap prevented him from getting into the pool first after the angel of the Lord stirred up the waters. Every time the man tried to get into the pool someone else would beat him to it; thus, day after day, week after week, month after month, and year after year the man never had a chance! How disheartening!

Scripture says when Jesus saw the man, "He knew that he already had been in that condition a long time." Jesus knows the terrible things someone has said about you, how you have been hurt, and what your deepest "sicknesses" are, too. He knows the desires of your heart. And He knows how long you may have been waiting to be healed.

"Do you want to be made well?" Jesus asked the man.

Jesus did not wait for the angel to come and stir the pool up. He didn't wait for the man to step into the pool before healing him. The Bible says Jesus commanded the man to take up his bed and walk, and immediately the man did!

Don't give up on your miracle! This man waited thirty-eight years to be healed! Jesus wants to make you well, too. If God has revealed an illness you didn't even realize you had, now is the time for God to set you free!

Heal me, O LORD, and I shall be healed; Save me, and I shall be saved, For You are my praise. — ***Jeremiah 17:14 (NKJV)***

CHAPTER TWENTY-SIX

In God's Appointed Time

See then that you walk circumspectly, not as fools but as wise, redeeming the time, because the days are evil. — ***Ephesians 5:15–16 (NKJV)***

One of the most interesting Greek words in the Bible is *kairos*, which means 'time' in Greek. However, *kairos* is a special kind of time—the right time—when momentous things happen or are about to happen. *Strong's Concordance* defines *kairos* as "a fixed and definite time" and "the time when things are brought to crisis, the decisive epoch waited for."[22] *Kairos* time is a biblical view of time.

One example of this kind of *kairos* time may be found in Galatians 4:4: "But when the fullness of time [*kairos*] had come, God sent forth his Son, born of woman, born under the law, to redeem those who were under the law, so that we might receive adoption as sons" (NKJV). God planned from the beginning that at a certain *kairos* moment, Jesus would be born. John the Baptist spoke of this kind of time when he said, "The time [*kairos*] is fulfilled, and the kingdom of God is at hand. Repent, and believe in the gospel." The moment you believed on Jesus as your Lord and Savior was a *kairos* moment.

Kairos time is different than *chronos* time, sixty minutes in an hour, twenty-four hours in a day, and seven days in a week. Consider the following quote:

> *Chronos* is clocks, deadlines, watches, calendars, agendas, planners, schedules, beepers. Chronos is time at her worst. Chronos keeps track. Chronos is the world's time.
>
> *Kairos* is transcendence, infinity, reverence, joy, passion, love, the Sacred. Kairos is intimacy with the Real. Kairos is time at her best. … Kairos is Spirit's time. — **Sarah Ban Breathnach**[23]

If we focus on *chronos* time, we might miss God's perfect opportunities Paul said we are charged to redeem (Ephesians 5:15–16). You will have opportune times and seasons set by God where He has designed for momentous things to come to fruition. These distinct moments of *kairos* time in your life will demand a response—'yes' or 'no'!

Stop looking at time as something that is slipping away and minutes you will never get back but as opportunities. Not every second holds the same value. Begin to shift your thinking to *kairos* time and you will never look at your days, weeks, months, and years the same way again!

Take heed, watch and pray; for you do not know when the time is. ***—Mark 13:33 (NKJV)***

CHAPTER TWENTY-SEVEN

Empowered to Be a Witness

And when He had said this, He breathed on them, and said to them, "Receive the Holy Spirit." ***— John 20:22 (NKJV)***

When a person is regenerated, bought by the blood of Jesus through the Holy Spirit, the Bible says they are "a new creation; old things have passed away; behold, all things have become new" (2 Corinthians 5:17 NKJV). When Jesus gave the Holy Spirit to his followers on resurrection day it was not the baptism in the Spirit as experienced at Pentecost (Acts 1:5; 2:4). It was rather an infusing of the disciples for the first time with the regenerating presence of the Holy Spirit and with new life from the risen Christ.

And they were all filled with the Holy Spirit and began to speak with other tongues, as the Spirit gave them utterance. ***— Acts 2:4 (NKJV)***

During Jesus' last discourse with the disciples before His trial and crucifixion, He promised them that His disciples would receive the Holy Spirit as the One who would regenerate them, saying, "He lives with you and will be in you" (John 14:17 NKJV).

Allow the Holy Spirit to reign and work in your life. There is work to be done and lost souls to win! The Holy Spirit will empower you to be a witness. The Holy Spirit gives life (Genesis 2:7; Ezekiel 37:9) and therefore will empower you to bring this life to others who desperately need it. You may feel ill-equipped, but the Holy Spirit will do the work; you need only to trust:

> Will God ever ask you to do something you are not able to do? The answer is yes—all the time! It must be that way, for God's glory and kingdom. If we function according to our ability alone, we get the glory; if we function according to the power of the Spirit within us, God gets the glory. He wants to reveal Himself to a watching world." — **Henry T. Blackaby**[24]

God is looking for saints who believe in His Word and are willing to step out on His Word to come alongside the contractor to complete the job!

> *But you shall receive power when the Holy Spirit has come upon you; and you shall be witnesses to Me in Jerusalem, and in all Judea and Samaria, and to the end of the earth.* **— *Acts 1:8 (NKJV)***

CHAPTER TWENTY-EIGHT

Insane for Jesus

So Jehu the son of Jehoshaphat, the son of Nimshi, conspired against Joram. (Now Joram had been defending Ramoth Gilead, he and all Israel, against Hazael king of Syria. But King Joram had returned to Jezreel to recover from the wounds which the Syrians had inflicted on him when he fought with Hazael king of Syria.) And Jehu said, "If you are so minded, let no one leave or escape from the city to go and tell it in Jezreel." So Jehu rode in a chariot and went to Jezreel, for Joram was laid up there; and Ahaziah king of Judah had come down to see Joram.

Now a watchman stood on the tower in Jezreel, and he saw the company of Jehu as he came, and said, "I see a company of men." And Joram said, "Get a horseman and send him to meet them, and let him say, 'Is it peace?'" So the horseman went to meet him, and said, "Thus says the king: 'Is it peace?'" And Jehu said, "What have you to do with peace? Turn around and follow me." So the watchman reported, saying, "The messenger went to them, but is not coming back." Then he sent out a second horseman who came to them, and said, "Thus says the king: 'Is it peace?'"

And Jehu answered, "What have you to do with peace? Turn around and follow me." So the watchman reported, saying, "He went up to them and is not coming back; and

> *the driving is like the driving of Jehu the son of Nimshi, for he drives furiously!"* — ***2 Kings 9:14–26 (NKJV)***

King Jehu, whose name means "Yahweh is he," was on a mission. He was purpose-driven, not self-driven. He was focused and determined to complete his assignment from God. 2 Kings 9:26 says Jehu was driving "furiously!" toward the watchmen in the tower in Jezreel. In today's language, we might say, "He was driving like a maniac!"

The word 'furiously' in the original Hebrew is the word *shiggaon,* and it means "craziness" or "madness." It is derived from a root word that means "to rave through insanity."[25]

Was Jehu insane? Not at all! Jehu was sent by God to cleanse the land from the house of evil Ahab, and he was a man on a mission. The watchmen who saw him coming couldn't make out exactly who they saw because Jehu was so passionate—his chariot was caught up in a bowl of dust! Now to be clear, Jehu's rage stemmed from his eager spirit to accomplish the mission he had been called to. He was submitted to God—a willing vessel to be used for God's glory. God has called us to a level of living that is God-purpose-driven, too. What does this look like in the life of a believer? Here are just a few ways followers of Jesus "drive furiously":

Through fervent prayer:

> Confess your trespasses to one another, and pray for one another, that you may be healed. The effective, fervent prayer of a righteous man avails much. (James 5:16 NKJV)

With a bold witness:

…for which I am an ambassador in chains; that in it I may speak boldly, as I ought to speak. (Ephesians 6:20 NKJV)

Passionate servitude:

No servant can serve two masters; for either he will hate the one and love the other, or else he will be loyal to the one and despise the other. You cannot serve God and mammon. (Luke 16:13 NKJV)

Merciful forgiveness:

For if you forgive men their trespasses, your heavenly Father will also forgive you. But if you do not forgive men their trespasses, neither will your Father forgive your trespasses. (Matthew 6:14–15 NKJV)

Passionate worship:

I beseech you therefore, brethren, by the mercies of God, that you present your bodies a living sacrifice, holy, acceptable to God, which is your reasonable service (Romans 12:1 NKJV)

CHAPTER TWENTY-NINE

God Is Able

And do not think to say to yourselves, "We have Abraham as our father." For I say to you that God is able to raise up children to Abraham from these stones. — ***Matthew 3:9 (NKJV)***

Abraham was one hundred years old, and Sarah was ninety when their son Isaac was born—a miracle to be sure! But this promise goes much deeper. God had promised Abraham that from him a great nation would come from him with descendants too great to number!

Today, the fulfillment of this can be seen in the Jewish people, the nation of Israel. Things that seem unrealistic or downright impossible are possible with God! He can do "exceedingly abundantly above all that we ask or think" (Ephesians 3:20 NKJV). However, we must trust that He can do what He says He can do.

- **Do you trust God to save you?** In the book of Daniel, Shadrach, Meshach, and Abednego knew God would save them from a flaming furnace that would have incinerated them if they even came near it! "If that is the case, our God whom we serve is able to deliver us from the burning fiery furnace, and He will deliver us from your hand, O king." The writer of Hebrews said, "He is able to save forever those who draw near" (Hebrews 7:25 NASB).

- **Do you trust God to make you stand?** The Greek word for 'stand' is *histémi*, and it means "to stand, place, set up, establish, [or] appoint."[26] It's a word that shows up often in relation to being able to resist Satan's attacks (Ephesians 6:11–14). "Who are you to judge another's servant? To his own master he stands or falls. Indeed, he will be made to stand, for God is able to make him stand" (Romans 14:4 NKJV).

- **Do you trust God to establish you?** "Now to Him who is able to establish you according to my gospel and the preaching of Jesus Christ…" (Romans 16:25 NKJV). The word 'establish' in Romans 16:25 is different than *histémi*. It is the word *stérizó* and it means "to strengthen," to "render constant," or "to turn resolutely in a certain direction."[27]

God promises to deliver you from evil, to help you resist Satan's attacks, and to help you remain constantly, resolutely turned toward Him. But you must trust Him! He promises He "is able to make all grace abound toward you, that you, always having all sufficiency in all things, may have an abundance for every good work" (2 Corinthians 9:8 NKJV) for those who ask. He is able, and He will do it.

If God can create a nation from an elderly, barren couple, He is able to work in your life, too.

> *...and being fully convinced that what He had promised He was also able to perform.* — ***Romans 4:21 (NKJV)***

CHAPTER THIRTY

Go Through It to Get to It

And He began to teach them that the Son of Man must suffer many things, and be rejected by the elders and chief priests and scribes, and be killed, and after three days rise again. He spoke this word openly. Then Peter took Him aside and began to rebuke Him. But when He had turned around and looked at His disciples, He rebuked Peter, saying, "Get behind Me, Satan! For you are not mindful of the things of God, but the things of men." When He had called the people to Himself, with His disciples also, He said to them, "Whoever desires to come after Me, let him deny himself, and take up his cross, and follow Me. For whoever desires to save his life will lose it, but whoever loses his life for My sake and the gospel's will save it. For what will it profit a man if he gains the whole world, and loses his own soul? Or what will a man give in exchange for his soul? For whoever is ashamed of Me and My words in this adulterous and sinful generation, of him the Son of Man also will be ashamed when He comes in the glory of His Father with the holy angels." — ***Mark 8:31–38 (NKJV)***

Jesus never said following Him would be easy. In fact, what could be easy about following a Savior who was crucified? There are things in life many of us probably wish were easier, too. But sometimes it is necessary to go through difficulties.

When Jesus told Peter He would have to go through a horrible death, Peter pushed back. He could not comprehend that Jesus had to do any more to be Savior, or go through suffering to prove He was the Messiah. It didn't make sense to Peter! But Jesus responded, lovingly, "Peter, get out of my way. Satan, get lost. You have no idea how God works" (Matthew 16:23 MSG).

Sometimes people have to go through things to get to where God wants them to be; more often than not, there are no shortcuts, either! Illnesses, unemployment, a terrible boss, a raging family member—these are all things that may seem unnecessary for spiritual growth, but God can see what you can't see. And as difficult as some situations might be, God's grace and mercy will undergird you and carry you to the other side. You can fight it, or embrace it like a soldier preparing for battle, knowing God is working all things for good. Anglican theologian Richard Sibbes writes that as "the winter prepares the earth for the spring, so do afflictions, sanctified, prepare the soul for glory."[28]

Whatever you are going through, there is nothing too big or too small to take to God. And remember, it's just a season. David, the greatest king who ever lived and likely one of the most persecuted, too, said this: "Weeping may endure for a night, but joy comes in the morning." (Psalm 30:5 NKJV). Winter will turn to spring; the dark of the night will dawn with the hope of a new day.

CHAPTER THIRTY-ONE

Hated for His Name…Again?

So they departed from the presence of the council, rejoicing that they were counted worthy to suffer shame for His name. — ***Acts 5:41 (NKJV)***

Sometimes it seems like no matter how hard you try to keep your halo straight, to never offend anyone or to keep your mouth zipped shut, you still are blamed or accused or ignored. However, this is a normal part of being a believer. When people look at you, interact with you or talk with you, without you realizing it, they are seeing Christ. And those who are not *for* Christ—those who are not yet believers—are against Him (Matthew 12:30).

It's important to remember that they are not against you! You represent Jesus, and this is whom their real issue is with. Jesus forewarned that this would happen, so don't be surprised when it does! The night before Jesus was crucified, while sharing a meal with His disciples, Jesus gives some of His parting words before leaving this earth—and some were difficult to swallow. For instance, He said:

> *If the world hates you, you know that it hated Me before it hated you. If you were of the world, the world would love its own. Yet because you are not of the world, but I chose you out of the world, therefore the world hates you.*
> ***— John 15:18–19 (NKJV)***

The people hated Jesus so much in His day that they crucified Him—and that hatred quickly extended to all Christians.

The prophet Isaiah also foretold believers would be hated, hundreds of years before Jesus was even born!

> *Hear the word of the LORD, you who tremble at His word: "Your brothers who hate you, who exclude you for My name's sake, Have said, 'Let the LORD be glorified, that we may see your joy.' But they will be put to shame." —* ***Isaiah 66:5 (NASB)***

But be encouraged! Isaiah gives the answer for why you may be experiencing hatred, persecution, even exclusion from groups. It is happening for His name's sake. The world's hatred of you is actually bringing glory to Him.

Thus, when you are persecuted or even hated, even though it might not make sense, know that it is bringing glory to your Father.

> How did Jesus expect His disciples to react under persecution (in Matthew 5:12)? "Rejoice and be glad!" We are not to retaliate like an unbeliever, nor sulk like a child, nor lick our wound in self-pity like a dog, nor just grin a bear it like a Stoic, still less pretend we enjoy it like a masochist. What then? We are to rejoice as a Christian should and even "leap for joy" (Luke 6:23). — **John Stott**[29]

Follow the example of Peter and the other Apostles in the book of Acts, who rejoiced "that they were counted worthy to suffer shame for His name" (Acts 5:41 NKJV).

> *I eagerly expect and hope that I will in no way be ashamed, but will have complete boldness, so that now as always Christ will be exalted in my body, whether by life or by death. —* ***1 Peter 4:16 (NIV)***

CHAPTER THIRTY-TWO

Fight for the Cause

And David said, "What have I done now? Is there not a cause? Then he turned from him toward another and said the same thing; and these people answered him as the first ones did. Now when the words which David spoke were heard, they reported them to Saul; and he sent for him. Then David said to Saul, "Let no man's heart fail because of him; your servant will go and fight with this Philistine."
— 1 Samuel 17:29–32 (NKJV)

Enemy "giants" are pursuing God's people, But the church seems to be burying its head in the sand.

One day, long before he was king, David's father Jesse called his young son and dispatched him on a pressing task. David was instructed to take food and ten kinds of cheese to his brothers and Saul's army captains in return for information about his brothers. Jesse wanted to know exactly how his boys were doing!

David learned the Israelite army was about to face one of its harshest enemies—the Philistines. Goliath was a soldier in that army, a giant of a man with massive armor. He boasted a bronze javelin on his back, a spear, and a sword, and even had a shield bearer who carried his shield. The Israelite army was frightened of this man who was almost ten feet tall!

The Israelite army was on their soil, having home court advantage, at a place that belonged to Judah, and they were ready to fight the Philistines. But every day Goliath the giant soldier would boldly defy Israel. Saul, the king of Judah, knew Israel did not have a man to match Goliath's size and strength, so Israel was "dismayed and greatly afraid" (1 Samuel 17:11 NKJV).

David responded, "Is there not a cause?" David proceeded to convince Saul to let him fight this giant in the land, despite the fact that he was a mere boy.

Is there not a cause today? The enemy is attacking families. Marriages are falling apart. Women are aborting innocent babies. And much of this is happening on God's turf—within the church. Believers claim to be followers of Christ and yet don't read their Bibles. And the church seems to be anemic and lethargic, lacking power, vigor, and vitality.

People are afraid of the "giants" in the land but forget that the God of Angel Armies is fighting the battle. Who will stand up and fight the giants, unafraid, like David?

> *Then David put his hand in his bag and took out a stone; and he slung it and struck the Philistine in his forehead, so that the stone sank into his forehead, and he fell on his face to the earth. —* ***1 Samuel 17:49 (NKJV)***

CHAPTER THIRTY-THREE

Get Your Junk out of Your Trunk

Therefore we also, since we are surrounded by so great a cloud of witnesses, let us lay aside every weight, and the sin which so easily ensnares us, and let us run with endurance the race that is set before us, looking unto Jesus, the author and finisher of our faith, who for the joy that was set before Him endured the cross, despising the shame, and has sat down at the right hand of the throne of God. — ***Hebrews 12:1–2 (NKJV)***

Your past is a pass to the future. But first you need to get the "junk out of your trunk."

Spiritual junk includes gambling, playing the lottery, dog track, bingo, casino, provocative dancing, fornicating, sex texting, pornography, drug and alcohol abuse, lying, cursing, adultery, homosexuality, and stealing. These things may be a part of your past, but it's time to let the past be the past. It's also time to move forward and to be guarded against repeating destructive, ungodly behaviors in the future.

Titus 2:12 teaches that the believer is to deny "ungodliness and worldly lusts" and "should live soberly, righteously, and godly in the present age" (NKJV). However, many believers hold on to the "3 Ms": memories, manners, and mistakes.

Past *memories* bring confusion. Past *manners* distort a person's walk with the Lord. And past *mistakes* suffocate potential. Instead, followers of Jesus need to break fellowship with any of these deceitful lies of the enemy:

> *And have no fellowship with the unfruitful works of darkness, but rather expose them. For it is shameful even to speak of those things which are done by them in secret. —* ***Ephesians 5:11–12 (NKJV)***

This means it's time to clean out the junk in your trunk. As 2 Timothy 2:21 says:

> *Therefore if anyone cleanses himself from the latter, he will be a vessel for honor, sanctified and useful for the Master, prepared for every good work.* ***(NKJV)***

The word for 'cleanse' in this verse is the Greek word *ekkathairó,* which is connected to a root word that means to purge or purify, as from literal or spiritual impurity.[30]

Purging yourself of the past will bring rest to your soul, relieving you from memories of past sin, shame, and guilt you may be hanging onto. You have already been redeemed and are free in Christ. Therefore, cut yourself off from past sin tendencies. God wants to sanctify you and move you toward the future *He* has planned for you—one that is pleasing to God, pure and grounded in truth.

But you, O man of God, flee from these things and pursue righteousness, godliness, faith, love, perseverance, and gentleness. — ***1 Timothy 6:11 (NKJV)***

CHAPTER THIRTY-FOUR

Broken and Beaten, but Blessed

And he arose that night and took his two wives, his two female servants, and his eleven sons, and crossed over the ford of Jabbok. He took them, sent them over the brook, and sent over what he had. Then Jacob was left alone; and a Man wrestled with him until the breaking of day. Now when He saw that He did not prevail against him, He touched the socket of his hip; and the socket of Jacob's hip was out of joint as He wrestled with him. And He said, "Let Me go, for the day breaks." But he said, "I will not let You go unless You bless me!" So He said to him, "What is your name?" He said, "Jacob." And He said, "Your name shall no longer be called Jacob, but Israel; for you have struggled with God and with men, and have prevailed." Then Jacob asked, saying, "Tell me Your name, I pray." And He said, "Why is it that you ask about My name?" And He blessed him there. So Jacob called the name of the place Peniel: "For I have seen God face to face, and my life is preserved." Just as he crossed over Penuel the sun rose on him, and he limped on his hip. — ***Genesis 32:22–31 (NKJV)***

"Lord, I need a car!"

Or maybe you need a husband, or a wife, or a job. Yet, how often do people ask, ask, ask of the Lord, but forget to thank Him for what they already have? How often do they acknowledge Him for His grace or sovereignty? Doing so requires a posture of being broken and beaten before the Lord; but doing so will also result in being blessed.

There is good news and bad news here. The good news is that God wants to bless His children abundantly more than they could ever imagine. But the bad news is that it's going to be a tough road.

Jacob had to wrestle all night long with an angel of the Lord, demanding his blessing (Genesis 32:22–31). There is a powerful lesson in this story. We, too, must be broken to be able to use God's blessings wisely, and for His glory. Sometimes this requires a long wrestling match with God. However, God will always win because He has His children's best interests at heart.

Jacob, whose name means "he deceives," had deceived many people, including Isaac (his father) and Esau (his twin brother). This was Jacob's favorite shortcut to gain blessings. It's possible that Jacob worshiped God out of his own selfish intents, too. But God was aware of Jacob's motivations and decided to adjust his focus.

While being chased by the men he had deceived, Jacob remembered God and acknowledged his futility. He prayed and asked God for help. God's blessing was more than Jacob could ever have imagined, but it didn't come in Jacob's lifetime. From Jacob and his descendants came a great nation. God was always only interested in Jacob's heart—that it would be broken and contrite before him. And He wants the same for you.

> *The sacrifices of God are a broken spirit, a broken and a contrite heart—these, O God, You will not despise.*
> ***— Psalm 51:17 (NKJV)***

CHAPTER THIRTY-FIVE

No Hiding from God

Can anyone hide himself in secret places, So I shall not see him?" says the LORD; "Do I not fill heaven and earth?" says the LORD. — ***Jeremiah 23:24 (NKJV)***

Most people are afraid to "expose" themselves before God, to lay all of their sin—even the darkest, most embarrassing iniquities—before God. Even though God says in Christ believers are cleansed and made "whiter than snow" (Psalm 51:7 NKJV) there is this innate human tendency to want to hide. Perhaps there is fear that secret sin will be unforgivable. However, no one can hide their sin from God. The prophet Jeremiah said God sees man "in secret places" (Jeremiah 23:24 NKJV) that mere human beings can't comprehend. These "secret places," *cether* in the original Hebrew,[31] are places where a person tries to hide, to carefully conceal what they don't want anyone to know.[32]

But God desires everything—every dark, ugly sin be laid at His feet so He can remove it "as far as the east is from the west!"

And if we are still unwilling, God's Word says that even then, "your sin will find you out..." (Numbers 32:23 NKJV). God will allow for it to be found out and dealt with. The book of Ecclesiastes says, "For God will bring every act to judgment, everything which is hidden, whether it is good or evil" (Ecclesiastes 12:14 NASB). Knowing that, confess your sin to God and allow Him to deal with it now! There is "nothing covered up that will not be revealed, nor hidden that will not be known" (Luke 12:2 NKJV).

There are many Christians who carry the burden of secret sins for years because they can't accept that God forgives and He forgets. I challenge you today to ask God to forgive you so you can be set free.

The writer of Hebrews said, "And there is no creature hidden from His sight, but all things are naked and open to the eyes of Him to whom we must give account" (Hebrews 4:13 NKJV). Don't be afraid to come out of the dark, and walk in the light of Jesus. He is waiting to cleanse you, so you might experience freedom!

> *If we confess our sins, He is faithful and just to forgive us our sins and to cleanse us from all unrighteousness.* ***— 1 John 1:9 (NKJV)***

CHAPTER THIRTY-SIX

God Is Our Refiner

I, the LORD, search the heart, I test the mind, even to give every man according to his ways, according to the fruit of his doings. — ***Jeremiah 17:10 (NKJV)***

The Bible says God is like a "refiner's fire" (Malachi 3:2). A refiner, in ancient biblical times, used fire to heat metal until it melted. He then skimmed away the impurities, or "dross" that would float to the top. Only then was the metal suitable to be made into usable vessels.

This imagery helps believers understand what it means when Scripture says God refines our souls. Alluding to this metal-refining process, the prophet Isaiah said, "Behold, I have refined you, but not as silver; I have tested you in the furnace of affliction" (Isaiah 48:10 NKJV). June Hunt writes that "dross" represents "anything that keeps us from being all that God wants us to be."[33] These "impurities" are sins that keeps us from being what God created us for.

God wants to purify us, and this imagery indicates the refining process is one that will not be easy. Often, a person will need to go through intense "heat" for the impurities and imperfections in their lives to, in a sense, "float to the surface" so they can be skimmed away. Like melted metal, what is left is pure. Solomon wrote, "Remove the dross from the silver, and a silversmith can produce a vessel" (Proverbs 25:4 NIV).

Why must God refine His people? God created man in His image, but because of sin, we fall short of God's glory. We are impure by our nature, but Pastor and author John Piper says that God "will have no alloys in heaven."[34]

This refinement process may come in the form of God's correction or discipline, or even affliction. David said in Psalm 119:71, however, that refinement, or affliction, "is good for me" (Psalm 119:71 NKJV) and that from it he "may learn Your statues" (Psalm 119:71 NKJV). God's process of refinement is never for destruction, but only for our good. It is through these refining periods in our life that God perfects us, makes us to be more like Christ, and transforms us into a vessel He can use for His purposes and His glory. Run to the Word of God and allow it to continue to purify you: "And the words of the Lord are flawless, like silver purified in a crucible, like gold refined seven times" (Psalm 12:6 NIV).

> *In this you greatly rejoice, though now for a little while, if need be, you have been grieved by various trials, that the genuineness of your faith, being much more precious than*

gold that perishes, though it is tested by fire, may be found to praise, honor, and glory at the revelation of Jesus Christ. — ***1 Peter 1:6–7 (NKJV)***

CHAPTER THIRTY-SEVEN

An Intercepted Blessing

So it was, when Jesus returned, that the multitude welcomed Him, for they were all waiting for Him. And behold, there came a man named Jairus, and he was a ruler of the synagogue. And he fell down at Jesus' feet and begged Him to come to his house, for he had an only daughter about twelve years of age, and she was dying. But as He went, the multitudes thronged Him. Now a woman, having a flow of blood for twelve years, who had spent all her livelihood on physicians and could not be healed by any came from behind and touched the border of His garment. And immediately her flow of blood stopped. And Jesus said, "Who touched Me?" When all denied it, Peter and those with him said, "Master, the multitudes throng and press You, and You say, 'Who touched Me?'" But Jesus said, "Somebody touched Me, for I perceived power going out from Me." Now when the woman saw that she was not hidden, she came trembling; and falling down before Him, she declared to Him in the presence of all the people the reason she had touched Him and how she was healed immediately. And He said to her, "Daughter, be of good cheer; your faith has made you well. Go in peace."
— Luke 8:40–48 (NKJV)

The word ‘interception’ means “to take, seize, or halt (someone or something on the way from one place to another); cut off from an intended destination”—as in intercepting a messenger.[35] Think of the game of football. An interception is when a quarterback throws the football to the wide receiver, but the ball in unexpectedly captured by the other team.

This is what happened to Jesus on his way to Jairus’s house to heal Jairus’s daughter. He was “cut off from an intended destination” by a woman with a bleeding problem. She had been sick for more than twelve years but was healed when she stopped Jesus in His tracks.

> *...touched the hem of His garment.* — ***Matthew 9:20 (NKJV)***

We can learn something from this woman, who had sought out doctors and spent all of her money trying to be healed. She did not wait for Jesus to come to her; she went to Him. On top of that, because of her bleeding problem, she was considered ceremonially unclean which affected her life both socially and spiritually. She was not allowed to fellowship with the public. She was not allowed to worship at the temple. She lived a life of solitude, as well as physical suffering.

Many people are unclean before the Lord, and need to run after Him for healing! They have been defiled by their sin and have no fellowship with God. They may attend the house of God, but they can’t worship because there is no relationship.

People spend their whole life searching for real joy and peace, but do not seek that one thing that could satisfy.

The world doesn't want you to seek Jesus for healing, forgiveness, or satisfaction. And yet, this is the only thing Jesus requires for healing! He says to you and to me, "Come to Me, all you who labor and are heavy laden, and I will give you rest" (Matthew 11:28 NKJV). Jesus told the woman it was her faith that healed her—faith alone. For those who believe, Jesus will forgive the sickness of sin and heal them body, soul, and spirit.

So you shall serve the LORD your God, and He will bless your bread and your water. And I will take sickness away from the midst of you. — ***Exodus 23:25 (NKJV)***

CHAPTER THIRTY-EIGHT

Let God Build Your "Wall"

Then Judah said, "The strength of the laborers is failing, and there is so much rubbish that we are not able to build the wall. And our adversaries said, 'They will neither know nor see anything, till we come into their midst and kill them and cause the work to cease.'" — ***Nehemiah 4:10–11 (NKJV)***

Nehemiah was an Israelite in Persian exile when he became vexed by the reports of the condition of Jerusalem. So he asked the pagan King Artaxerxes if he could go to Jerusalem to repair the city, and miraculously, the king gave him permission to do it.

Initially, the Hebrew people were excited and worked hard to rebuild Jerusalem's wall. However, they seemed to lose steam, or momentum. Nehemiah 4:10 indicates the people were worn out, discouraged, and defeated.

Israel's enemies convinced the Israelites they would never finish, or that they would finish and immediately be taken captive again, saying, "They will neither know nor see anything, till we come into their midst and kill them and cause the work to cease" (Nehemiah 4:11 NKJV). Likely they were discouraged and allowed these lies to affect their morale.

Unfortunately, this often happens in the body of Christ, too. People will be on fire for the Lord one day, and then a month later they sputter and fall and never reach their full potential. They listen to the voice of the enemy more than the voice of God. And they lose strength and sputter out on their callings.

The only way to regain strength and keep the momentum going, especially when the "job" gets difficult is to remember the believer's strength comes from the Lord alone. Paul reminded the Philippians that they could "do all things through Christ who strengthens" (Philippians 4:13 NKJV), and Isaiah wrote that God "gives power to the weak, and to those who have no might He increases strength" (Isaiah 40:29 NKJV).

But Israel pressed on. Fifty-two days from the day they started, Israel completed the wall. Nehemiah's enemies heard about it and the surrounding nations saw it and were disheartened. Why? Nehemiah said it was because "they perceived that this work was done by our God" (Nehemiah 6:16b NKJV).

You have been called to do extraordinary things in the kingdom! Take the first step, start moving, and keep the momentum going but first, lean on God for strength. Pick up your tools, pick up your mortar and bricks, and get to work! Finish the task at hand; let God build your wall.

Finally, my brethren, be strong in the Lord and in the power of His might. — **Ephesians 6:10 (NKJV)**

CHAPTER THIRTY-NINE

Holy to the Lord

You shall also make a plate of pure gold and engrave on it, like the engraving of a signet: HOLINESS TO THE LORD.
— Exodus 28:36 (NKJV)

People throw around the word 'holy' often, and though they don't mean disrespect, it is likely they don't have a biblical understanding of what a reverent word it is. Consider how many times you've heard, "Holy guacamole!" or "Holy cow!"

Let's look at the Hebrew word for 'holiness,' *qodesh*. *Qodesh* means "apartness" or "sacredness."[36] It is a word referring to a person, item, or even a piece of land set apart for God's use. The sanctuary in the tabernacle that the high priest ministered in was called "the holy place."

But God's desire for things and places to be holy is only a picture or a shadow of what He desires for His people.

God created man in His image—and He is a holy, righteous, perfect God. "Exalt the LORD our God, and worship at His holy hill; for the LORD our God is holy!" the psalmist sang (Psalm 99:9 NKJV). When man sinned in the garden, his spirit was marred—that holy image of God was darkened by sin, and God could not be in sin's presence.

But since the beginning, God had a plan for restoration. It would be through a Savior, the seed of the woman (Genesis 3:15), through Abraham's son Isaac, in the line of Judah, that a Savior would be born. This Savior would "crush the head of the serpent" (see Genesis 3:15), ending Satan's reign on earth and rectifying the issue of holiness.

However, while living on earth the believer must walk this out every day. God calls us to be "holy, for I am holy" (NKJV). Until we reach heaven, however, we will still wrestle with our fallen nature which will always try to get us to be anything but holy. Because of the blood of Jesus, when God looks at the believer, He sees only the perfect holiness of Christ. This is who the believer is, and this is what the believer was made to be:

> *For you are a holy people to the LORD your God; the LORD your God has chosen you to be a people for Himself, a special treasure above all the peoples on the face of the earth.* — ***Deuteronomy 7:6 (NKJV)***

God desires us to be holy, to be "separate" from the world, so that when people look at us they see Jesus. Our lives should be a living witness to the existence of God!

And you shall be holy to Me, for I the LORD am holy, and have separated you from the peoples, that you should be Mine. — ***Leviticus 20:26 (NKJV)***

CHAPTER FOURTY

Get Out of the Pit!

So it came to pass, when Joseph had come to his brothers, that they stripped Joseph of his tunic, the tunic of many colors that was on him. Then they took him and cast him into a pit. And the pit was empty; there was no water in it. And they sat down to eat a meal. Then they lifted their eyes and looked, and there was a company of Ishmaelites, coming from Gilead with their camels, bearing spices, balm, and myrrh, on their way to carry them down to Egypt. So Judah said to his brothers, "What profit is there if we kill our brother and conceal his blood? Come and let us sell him to the Ishmaelites, and let not our hand be upon him, for he is our brother and our flesh." And his brothers listened. Then Midianite traders passed by; so the brothers pulled Joseph up and lifted him out of the pit, and sold him to the Ishmaelites for twenty shekels of silver. And they took Joseph to Egypt. ***Genesis 37:23–28 (NKJV)***

Joseph was in a pretty dark pit, literally. His brothers (minus Reuben, who was absent when the plan was hatched) were heavy with hatred and jealousy toward him, for Joseph was his father's favorite. They threw him into a water cistern, only to pull him out and sell him to the Egyptians.

Water cisterns in ancient biblical times were often carved out of limestone bedrock, or dug deep into the ground and lined with some sort of plaster. They held water for the dry months when there was no rain. It was likely dark, very wet, full of mire, and scary.

Sometimes these water cisterns were used as dungeons or prisons, as in the case of Jeremiah:

> *So they took Jeremiah and cast him into the dungeon of Malchiah the king's son, which was in the court of the prison, and they let Jeremiah down with ropes. And in the dungeon there was no water, but mire. So Jeremiah sank in the mire. — **Jeremiah 38:6 (NKJV)***

Have you ever felt like you were sinking in the mire—like you were in a deep, dark pit with no way out? David wrote in Psalm 35, "Without cause they have hidden their net for me in a pit…" (Psalm 35:7 NKJV). A pit may be a place of depression, grief, anger, or resentment. But God says He will be the one to "pull you out," and promises to give you a firm place to stand when He does.

Remember that though you may be in a pit and feeling attacked, oppressed, or depressed, this is not where you are meant to be—and it is not where you will always be. You are not meant to live in the pit. Seek the one who can pull you out, and trust Him to do it!

He also brought me up out of a horrible pit, out of the miry clay, and set my feet upon a rock, and established my steps.
— Psalm 40:2 (NKJV)

CHAPTER FOURTY-ONE

Worship God in Tears

I am weary with my groaning; All night I make my bed swim; I drench my couch with my tears. My eye wastes away because of grief; It grows old because of all my enemies. ***— Psalm 6:6 (NKJV)***

How is it possible to worship God after receiving a doctor's bad report? How is it possible to worship God when you don't have two pennies to rub together? Anybody can worship when the battle is *over.* Anybody can praise God when a sickness is healed, when a marriage is restored, when a family is mended, when the retirement account is fat, and when there is money in the bank. When things are going well, it's natural to give credit to God! But what about the tough times? How is it possible then?

It is possible! In fact, God tells us it blesses Him when we do. In challenging times, we can worship God with our tears. It may not be pretty worship—in fact, it will probably be ugly, messy, and displeasing in appearance. But God sees worship through tears and our hearts.

God wants you to worship in tears and groans, when your heart is broken and with bloodshot eyes. He wants honor even when your life doesn't make sense, and when you feel alone, lost and sad. This is how God's children show faith in God, in times of distress.

Consider Job. He had lost everything—his wealth, his family, *everything*. But in the middle of his deep loss, he rose, rent his mantle, shaved his head, and fell to the ground and worshipped God:

> *Naked I came from my mother's womb, and naked shall I return there. The LORD gave, and the LORD has taken away; blessed be the name of the LORD.* — ***Job 1:21 (NKJV)***

Job worshipped God with a broken heart and through intense pain and confusion. He didn't know why his world was snatched away from him, but still He praised God. Job's act of worship kept him connected to the purpose God had for him that he was not able to see in that moment. When we worship out of our deep grief, through tears, God sees. The psalmist said, "The eyes of the LORD are on the righteous, and his ears are attentive to their cry…" (Psalm 34:15 NIV). Trudy Metzger writes:

> I will continue to weep shamelessly for our churches, our communities, our nation, and the nations around. When you see me cry, I'm not "losing it". I'm not overwhelmed. I'm

> simply trusting God to carry what I cannot. I will worship God with my tears.[37]

Will you do the same?

One day, we will worship God with no tears! Weeping may "stay for the night, but rejoicing comes in the morning…" (Psalm 30:5 NKJV). One day, when Jesus rules and reigns from Jerusalem, He will wipe every tear from every eye!

> *And God will wipe away every tear from their eyes; there shall be no more death, nor sorrow, nor crying. There shall be no more pain, for the former things have passed away."*
> ***— Revelation 21:4 (NKJV)***

CHAPTER FOURTY-TWO

Your Words Have Power

*A fool's lips enter into contention, and his mouth calls for blows. A fool's mouth is his destruction, and his lips are the snare of his soul. — **Proverbs 18:6–7 (NKJV)***

There is power in words!

The enemy knows this and tries to manipulate our words to try "to steal, and to kill, and to destroy" (John 10:10 NKJV). He uses words to try to derail the "gospel train" believers are riding on. One little pebble can cause a train to jump its tracks, causing destruction and even death. So can words. Words can bring life, but unfortunately, words can also speak death. (James 3:10).

James, the half-brother of Jesus, wrote that the tongue "is a fire, a world of iniquity. The tongue is so set among our members that it defiles the whole body, and sets on fire the course of nature; and it is set on fire by hell" (James 3:6 NKJV). He compares controlling speech to putting a bit in a horse's mouth—when controlled, it can "bridle the whole body…" (James 3:2 NKJV). The word 'bridle' is a long Greek word, *chalinagógeó*. *Chalinagógeó* means "to guide" or to "hold in check, restrain."[38]

But James also wrote that *no man* can tame the tongue, which is "unruly, evil, full of deadly poison…" (James 3:8 NKJV). How then are we to tackle this issue? Even Scripture says bridling the tongue is impossible!

Just a few verses later, still teaching about controlling the tongue, James hinted at an answer: "If you have bitter envy and self-seeking in your hearts, do not boast and lie against the truth" (James 3:14 NKJV). The apostle Matthew clarifies this even further:

> *But those things which proceed out of the mouth come from the heart, and they defile a man. For out of the heart proceed evil thoughts, murders, adulteries, fornications, thefts, false witness, blasphemies. These are the things which defile a man, but to eat with unwashed hands does not defile a man.* — ***Matthew 15:18–19 (NKJV)***

To tame the tongue, we must first deal with sin stored up in our heart. Our mouth is the airplane and our navigation (GPS) is our heart. Before we can bridle our tongue, we must deal with what's in our hearts.

Are you struggling with controlling your tongue? It takes the power of Jesus Christ, and it begins with your heart. Examine it, confess areas of sin—such as bitterness, envy, or hate—and allow God to heal you of those emotions. Ask Him to transform your heart—and you will see a change in your speech!

Let no corrupt word proceed out of your mouth, but what is good for necessary edification, that it may impart grace to the hearers. — ***Ephesians 4:29 (NKJV)***

CHAPTER FOURTY-THREE

Get into Position

In the second year of King Darius, in the sixth month, on the first day of the month, the word of the LORD came by Haggai the prophet to Zerubbabel the son of Shealtiel, governor of Judah, and to Joshua the son of Jehozadak, the high priest, saying, "Thus speaks the LORD of hosts, saying: 'This people says, "The time has not come, the time that the LORD'S house should be built." Then the word of the LORD came by Haggai the prophet, saying, "Is it time for you yourselves to dwell in your paneled houses, and this temple to lie in ruins?" Now therefore, thus says the LORD of hosts: "Consider your ways! "You have sown much, and bring in little; you eat, but do not have enough; you drink, but you are not filled with drink; you clothe yourselves, but no one is warm; and he who earns wages, earns wages to put into a bag with holes." Thus says the LORD of hosts: "Consider your ways! Go up to the mountains and bring wood and build the temple, that I may take pleasure in it and be glorified," says the LORD. — ***Haggai 1:1–8 (NKJV)***

Haggai was a prophet of God during the time the Israelites were building the second temple in Jerusalem. Haggai came to the governor of Judah, not the king, because there was no king ruling Judah at that time.

Notice in Haggai 1:1–8 alone, God is referred to as "the LORD of hosts" three times (Haggai 1:7 NKJV). This is not by accident. The word 'hosts' is a translation of the Hebrew word *sabaóth*, which means "armies."[39] This imagery of God as the Commander of angel armies sets the context for what Haggai is prophesying about—and it's not only about the construction of a building. Rather, *it is the foundational step to God's battle plan.*

God says, "Consider your ways! Go up to the mountains and bring wood and build the temple, that I may take pleasure in it and be glorified" (Haggai 1:7–8 NKJV). Building the temple is the first step in winning any battle.

The temple of the Lord was the place God designated that His people would come to worship him. And worship must come before everything. It is as if God is saying, "Get into position! Prepare for battle!" Our battle is not against flesh and blood, against mere people or nations. No, our battle is "against principalities, against powers, against the rulers of the darkness of this age, against spiritual hosts of wickedness in the heavenly places" (Ephesians 6:12 NKJV).

Did you catch that word 'hosts' in Ephesians 6:12? Our battle is against *spiritual armies* of wickedness that we cannot see with our eyes. Worship is spiritual warfare. And spiritual wars cannot be won with physical weapons. Paul wrote to the Corinthians, "For the weapons of our warfare are not carnal, but mighty through God to the pulling down of strong holds" (2 Corinthians 10:4 (NKJV).

A person who is praising God cannot hate at the same time. A person who is thanking God cannot be bitter. A person can't worship and be tempted to sin. Worship is thus the believer's most powerful weapon in his or her arsenal!

If you are longing for victory over a particular sin, begin by "going up to the mountains and bring wood and build the temple." Begin with worship and enemy armies will scatter!

Oh come, let us worship and bow down; Let us kneel before the LORD our Maker. — ***Psalm 95:6 (NKJV)***

CHAPTER FOURTY-FOUR

Second Chances

Do not remember the former things, nor consider the things of old. Behold, I will do a new thing. — ***Isaiah 43:18–19 (NKJV)***

God is a God of second chances:

- Jacob was a deceiver; *but*
- Peter had a bad temper; *but*
- David committed adultery and murder; *but*
- Noah got drunk; *but*
- Jonah hid from God; *but*
- Paul killed innocent Christians; *but*
- Gideon was a rebel; *but*
- Miriam spoke behind her brother's back; *but*
- Martha was a busy-body; *but*
- Mary Magdalene was a prostitute; *but*
- Thomas doubted; *but*
- Sarah was impatient; *but*
- Esau was a sell-out; *but*

- Zacchaeus was short and robbed people; *but…*

God gave them all second chances. God forgives sin, and He forgets it. If God only chose people who got it right the first time, there would be nobody to choose, for as the Scriptures tell us, "All have sinned and fall short of the glory of God…" (Romans 3:23 NKJV). The Bible includes story after story of men and women who received second chances. In fact, many received third and fourth chances. According to the Message translation of Psalm 30:2–3, David said, "GOD, my God, I yelled for help and you put me together. GOD, you pulled me out of the grave, gave me another chance at life when I was down-and-out" (MSG).

However, God's patience and forgiveness has a limit. Paul wrote in Romans 1:18–32 that when people continue to spurn God's patience, turn a deaf ear, and ignore His call to repent, our hearts will eventually grow hard toward Him. We must confess our sin to Him, trusting His faithfulness to forgive it, but like Jesus told the woman at the well, "Go and sin no more" (John 8:11 NKJV).

Beloved Christian author Karen Kingsbury writes in her book *Oceans Apart*:

> I tell of hearts and souls and dances…
>
> Butterflies and second chances;
>
> Desperate ones and dreamers bound,
>
> Seeking life from barren ground,

Who suffer on in earthly fate
The bitter pain of agony hate,
Might but they stop and here forgive
Would break the bonds to breathe and live
And find that God in goodness brings
A chance for change, the hope of wings
To rest in Him, and self to die
And so become a butterfly.[40]

Do you need a second chance? Ask Him.

The Lord is not slack concerning His promise, as some count slackness, but is longsuffering toward us, not willing that any should perish but that all should come to repentance. — ***2 Peter 3:9 (NKJV)***

CHAPTER FOURTY-FIVE

Spiritual Schizophrenia

If any of you lacks wisdom, let him ask of God, who gives to all liberally and without reproach, and it will be given to him. But let him ask in faith, with no doubting, for he who doubts is like a wave of the sea driven and tossed by the wind. For let not that man suppose that he will receive anything from the Lord; he is a double-minded man, unstable in all his ways. — ***James 1:5–8 (NKJV)***

One major problem believers in Jesus Christ have today is also the same major problem first century Christians struggled with two thousand years ago: being "double-minded."

Being "double-minded" comes from a Greek word *dipsuchos*, which means to waver, to be uncertain, or to doubt, or to be "divided in interest."[41] In the Bible, James 1:8 says a "double-minded man, unstable in all his ways" (NKJV). But what does it really mean to be double-minded?

Being double-minded is when a person knows what they should do, but later that day (or even that hour) finds himself or herself doing the exact opposite. If this happens to you quite frequently, it isn't clinical schizophrenia. Rather, it's more like spiritual schizophrenia.

Paul was familiar with spiritual schizophrenia. He wrote:

> *For what I am doing, I do not understand. For what I will to do, that I do not practice; but what I hate, that I do. If, then, I do what I will not to do, I agree with the law that it is good. But now, it is no longer I who do it, but sin that dwells in me. For I know that in me (that is, in my flesh) nothing good dwells; for to will is present with me, but how to perform what is good I do not find. For the good that I will to do, I do not do; but the evil I will not to do, that I practice. Now if I do what I will not to do, it is no longer I who do it, but sin that dwells in me. — **Romans 7:15–20 (NKJV)***

Double-minded believers are always torn in two different directions. They compromise God's best for what the world says is best. They are led by the Spirit—some of the time. They give into past addictions or habits quickly. However, God says there is no place for double-mindedness in the Bible. Titus 2:12 teaches believers to deny ungodliness and worldly lusts and to "live soberly, righteously, and godly in the present age" (NKJV). God is clear we are to live with a mind focused on righteousness.

Isaiah 29:13 described Israel's double-mindedness this way: "Inasmuch as these people draw near with their mouths and honor Me with their lips, but have removed their hearts far from Me, and their fear toward Me is taught by the commandment of men" (Isaiah 29:13 NKJV). The people of Israel would say certain things, but their hearts were far from God. In modern-day language, they were paying God 'lip service.'

Do you find yourself divided in word and deed? Do you give God lip service around certain people while acting differently around others? Confess this to God, and ask Him to create in you a clean heart and give you a renewed Spirit.

Cleanse your hands, you sinners; and purify your hearts, you double-minded. — ***James 4:8 (NKJV)***

CHAPTER FOURTY-SIX

When Nothing Makes Sense

Then Joseph's master took him and put him into the prison, a place where the king's prisoners were confined. And he was there in the prison. But the LORD was with Joseph and showed him mercy, and He gave him favor in the sight of the keeper of the prison. And the keeper of the prison committed to Joseph's hand all the prisoners who were in the prison; whatever they did there, it was his doing. The keeper of the prison did not look into anything that was under Joseph's authority, because the Lord was with him; and whatever he did, the LORD made it prosper. — ***Genesis 39:20–23 (NKJV)***

Joseph was placed in prison not for doing anything wrong, but for doing something right. Many reading this may relate—feeling persecuted for doing the right thing. It's one thing to be in trouble for something you *have* done, but to be in trouble for what *others* have done is another story.

When this happens, the first thing people tend to do is demand that God help them understand why. But God asks us to do something different: *trust Him.*

Trust in the LORD with all your heart, and lean not on your own understanding; in all your ways acknowledge Him, and He shall direct your paths. — ***Proverbs 3:5–6 (NKJV)***

The apostle Paul was perplexed at times, yet he trusted God. Joseph couldn't understand what good could come from being thrown in prison, yet he found himself overseeing all of the other prisoners. And the most profound thing about this story? Scripture say the keeper of the jail gave Joseph all authority "because the LORD was with him" (1 Samuel 18:14 NIV).

The same God who was with Joseph in the good times was with him in the bad times!

Be willing to wait and see how God is knitting good things and bad things together for "His purpose" (Romans 8:28 NKJV). Eventually, Pharaoh put Joseph in charge of the whole land of Egypt and even gave Joseph his signet ring—a sign of absolute authority. When Joseph's entire family came to Egypt during the famine, Joseph was able to care for them because of his place of authority. Seeing God's sovereignty over his life, he was able to declare that though his brothers meant to harm him, "God meant it for good, in order to bring it about as it is this day, to save many people alive" (Genesis 50:20 NKJV).

When nothing makes sense, God has perfect sense.

Great is our Lord, and mighty in power; His understanding is infinite. — ***Psalm 147:5 (NKJV)***

CHAPTER FOURTY-SEVEN

Take Part in the Harvest

And He said, "The kingdom of God is as if a man should scatter seed on the ground, and should sleep by night and rise by day, and the seed should sprout and grow, he himself does not know how. For the earth yields crops by itself: first the blade, then the head, after that the full grain in the head. But when the grain ripens, immediately he puts in the sickle, because the harvest has come." — ***Mark 4:26–29 (NKJV)***

Jesus tells a parable, a story to help His listeners understand a deeper spiritual truth, about planting and harvesting. There is a stage in farming called germination, at which point the planted seed awakens from dormancy and begins to sprout. The growth process of the seed from this point on is steady, continual, and slow.

This is like the growth of the believer. Each step in the growth process is important—vital—and it all leads to the final stage: the harvest.

Jesus teaches this parable to instruct His listeners that growth comes from consuming the Word of God. The prophet Isaiah uses this agricultural imagery, too, saying:

> *For as the rain comes down, and the snow from heaven, and do not return there, but water the earth, and make it bring forth and bud, that it may give seed to the sower and bread to the eater, so shall My word be that goes forth from My mouth; it shall not return to Me void, but it shall accomplish what I please, and it shall prosper in the thing for which I sent it.* — ***Isaiah 55:10–11 (NKJV)***

For plants to grow, water is essential. For believers to grow, "rain"—or the Word of God—is critical. God's Word goes out, spoken and written, and never returns void. It accomplishes what it is sent to do. According to the parable of the kingdom of God, this is what Jesus meant by "the full grain in the head." At that point, the harvest is imminent!

Look out and see the many stages of the harvest. Some people are mere seeds that are beginning to sprout. Some are in the growth stage, waiting for the ripening stage. And many are ready for harvest. And each believer is called to participate, whether by sharing the gospel with unbelievers, calling people to make a decision for Christ, or discipling believers—all the while sharing and teaching the Word of God.

> *Do you not say, "There are still four months and then comes the harvest"? Behold, I say to you, lift up your eyes and look at the fields, for they are already white for harvest! And he who reaps receives wages, and gathers*

fruit for eternal life, that both he who sows and he who reaps may rejoice together. For in this the saying is true: "One sows and another reaps." — ***John 4:35–37 (NKJV)***

CHAPTER FOURTY-EIGHT

Are You Still Holding On?

Then she arose with her daughters-in-law that she might return from the country of Moab, for she had heard in the country of Moab that the LORD had visited His people by giving them bread. Therefore she went out from the place where she was, and her two daughters-in-law with her; and they went on the way to return to the land of Judah. And Naomi said to her two daughters-in-law, "Go, return each to her mother's house. The LORD deal kindly with you, as you have dealt with the dead and with me. The LORD grant that you may find rest, each in the house of her husband." So she kissed them, and they lifted up their voices and wept. And they said to her, "Surely we will return with you to your people." But Naomi said, "Turn back, my daughters; why will you go with me? Are there still sons in my womb, that they may be your husbands? Turn back, my daughters, go—for I am too old to have a husband. If I should say I have hope, if I should have a husband tonight and should also bear sons, would you wait for them till they were grown? Would you restrain yourselves from having husbands? No, my daughters; for it grieves me very much for your sakes that the hand of the LORD has gone out against me!" Then they lifted up their voices and wept again; and Orpah kissed her mother-in-law, but Ruth clung to her. And she said, "Look, your sister-in-law has gone back to her people and to her gods; return after your sister-in-law." But Ruth said: "Entreat me not to leave you, or to

> *turn back from following after you; for wherever you go, I will go; and wherever you lodge, I will lodge; your people shall be my people, and your God, my God."* ***— Ruth 1:6–16 (NKJV)***

Most people have experienced, or will have an experience, with transition regarding the promises and purposes of God in their life. In fact, it is likely you may be going through something major in your life at this very moment. When this happens, there are two choices: To let go, or to hold on.

Naomi, Ruth, and Orpah were in transition. When each of their husbands died, Naomi—Ruth and Orpah's mother-in-law—decided to return to Israel. Orpah "let go" and decided to remain in Moab, a nation without God. Conversely, Ruth stayed with Naomi. She left her family and culture behind her in Moab to follow her mother-in-law to Israel, husbandless. Ruth vowed to follow Naomi and come under the God of Israel's protection (Ruth 1:16–17) in one of the greatest examples of loyalty in all of history.

But Ruth and Naomi's transition didn't end there. When they arrived in Bethlehem, Ruth experienced feeling like an outcast, as she was a foreigner to Israel. And Naomi was a stranger to her own people! It was likely disheartening, and surely along the way Ruth doubted ever leaving the comfort of Moab. However, this transition lead to Ruth's marriage to Boaz, and the birth of a baby boy who would end up being the great-grandfather to the Messiah—Jesus!

The greatest temptation during a season of transition is to become discouraged and give up. However, you may miss a blessing beyond your wildest imagination if you do.

> *Have I not commanded you? Be strong and of good courage; do not be afraid, nor be dismayed, for the LORD your God is with you wherever you go.* — ***Joshua 1:9 (NKJV)***

CHAPTER FOURTY-NINE

The Best Is Yet to Come

He who has begun a good work in you will complete it until the day of Jesus Christ. — ***Philippians 1:6 (NKJV)***

God is progressive. He moves His people forward in a direction that points toward a future destiny.

To be progressive means "proceeding step by step";[42] it can indicate growth, development, or advancement.

When God called Abram in Genesis 12, He told him, "I am going to make your name great. I'm going to bless you. I'm going to make you a great nation." What promises! It is likely Abraham had difficulty figuring out how to internalize this info. Abraham was an ordinary guy, called out of the pagan world by God and given promises that didn't make sense. But God was true to His Word. He only trusted and obeyed God, and God did the rest.

When God sets out to do something, it is not predicated upon those that don't believe but only rests on those that do believe. Abram believed God, and Scripture says it was credited to him as righteousness. This means though Abraham didn't know Jesus, his belief in God's promises saved him.

God has made promises to you, too! Scripture is full of them. He has pledged those who believe in Jesus Christ eternal life in a good land. He has promised rest to those who trust in Him. He has covenanted He will never leave or abandon those who call on His name. Some promises are easy to trust in; others, like the promises made to Abraham, are more difficult. For example, God has promised He has a purpose for each person on this earth—a mission of sorts. For many who are still wrestling with past sin, issues of insecurity, hard-to-break habits or even sickness, this might be hard to grasp.

But God promises through Paul in Philippians 1:6 that He is the one who began a good work in you, and He is the one who will complete it. You may not be able to see how, just as Abraham couldn't see. But He will complete it! That word 'complete' in Greek is *epiteleō*. It means "to bring to an end, accomplish, perfect, execute, [or] complete." It also means "to take upon one's self."[43]

God is taking it upon Himself to complete the work He started in you, so that you will be perfected for the day of Christ!

...who will also confirm you to the end, that you may be blameless in the day of our Lord Jesus Christ. — ***1 Corinthians 1:8 (NKJV)***